MELVILLE'S ART OF DEMOCRACY

MELVILLE'S
ART OF
DEMOCRACY

Nancy Fredricks

THE UNIVERSITY OF GEORGIA PRESS
Athens & London

© 1995 by The University of Georgia Press
Athens, Georgia 30602
All rights reserved
Designed by Walton Harris
Set in Adobe Garamond by Tseng Information Systems, Inc.
Printed and bound by Braun-Brumfield, Inc.

The paper in this book meets the guidelines for permanence and durability
of the Committee on Production Guidelines for Book Longevity
of the Council on Library Resources.

Printed in the United States of America
99 96 97 98 99 C 5 4 3 2 1

Library of Congress Cataloging in Publication Data
Fredricks, Nancy.
Melville's art of democracy / Nancy Fredricks.
p.   cm.
Includes bibliographical references (p.) and index.
ISBN 0-8203-1682-2 (alk. paper)
1. Melville, Herman, 1819–1891 — Political and social views.
2. Politics and literature — United States — History — 19th century.
3. Political fiction, American — History and criticism.
4. Democracy in literature.   I. Title.
PS2388.P6F74   1995
813'.3 — dc20   94-15272

British Library Cataloging in Publication Data available

to
"thou just Spirit of Equality"

CONTENTS

ACKNOWLEDGMENTS

I thank Marc Shell for introducing me to Melville through *Pierre,* Martin Pops for generously sharing with me his wealth of Melvillean knowledge, and Rodolphe Gasche for bringing philosophical texts to life with tireless dedication. My thanks also to another of my teachers, Leslie Fiedler, whose passion for literature and democracy has had a profound impact on my ideas of teaching and scholarship. I am grateful for the work and support of Susan Howe and Carolyn Karcher, two of my beloved sisters in Melville studies. My deepest gratitude goes to Carolyn Karcher and H. Bruce Franklin for reading the manuscript and offering thoughtful suggestions and invaluable encouragement. In fond memory of Nancy K. Hill, I express my appreciation to the members of the Humanities Department and the University of Colorado for supporting interdisciplinary and comparative studies in the arts. Thanks also to my parents for sharing their love of music, reading, and justice, and for contributing to my class-consciousness. Finally, I thank John Bryant, Robert K. Wallace, Gabriel Pearson, Bill Warner, Newton Garver, Carol Jacobs, Jill Robbins, Martin Bickman, Leland Krauth, the people at the University of Georgia Press, and all those friends who have inspired, challenged, and supported me.

An earlier version of chapter 9 appeared in *Studies in American Fiction* 19, no. 1 (Spring 1991): 41–54.

INTRODUCTION

1

THE ART OF
DEMOCRACY

OF ALL THE IDEAS that I hope to convey to my readers, foremost is the relevance of Melville's writings for those of us working toward greater democratization of cultural and literary studies. When Melville took upon himself the task of bringing "republican progressiveness into Literature," he had to deal with many of the same problems we face in our profession today concerning marginalization based on class, ethnicity, gender, and sexual preference, and the relationship between politics and theoretical discourse. This book's general purpose is to identify and analyze various theoretical positions represented in Melville's work that bear on the relation between democratic values and artistic-critical practice. Of particular interest is Melville's engagement with issues of class, popular culture, feminism, and aesthetics in *Moby-Dick, Pierre,* and several of his short stories.[1] Topics addressed include Melville's sympathetic treatment of the tinhorn rebellion of tenant farmers protesting the patroon feudalism in upstate New York, his use of the generic elements of nineteenth-century melodrama, his attempts to address women readers, and his interpretation of America's fascination with sublime aesthetics and its relation to German transcendentalism. These previously neglected and often misunderstood aspects of Melville's work reflect his sympathies with the radical-democrat movement and his desire to create an art that takes into account what he calls the "difference" made by the Declaration of Independence (*Letters,* 80).[2]

This book has a dual focus. *Moby-Dick* and *Pierre,* Melville's two most ambitious and expansive prose works, are read in relation to one another as forming a giant diptych, with each half equivalent in scope and scale, linked together formally and thematically by a common concern with exploring the ethical and political implications of the limits to our powers of representation. Melville's marking of those limits is not merely an act of nihilism; it is part of his attempt to create an art that embodies egalitarian and multicultural democratic values.

On a formal level, Melville marks the limits to representation by his use of such devices as the oxymoron, diptych structure, dramatic form, and collage. These structures of multiplicity work in Melville's texts to decenter discourse and open a space for various perspectives and voices. On a thematic level, Melville explores limits to representation in his engagement with sublime aesthetics, his critique of typology and fanaticism, his representations of marginalized women, his valorization of music as a nonrepresentational art form, and his generic interest in melodrama, a form that valorizes music and that, in Melville's time, represented the interests of the unrepresented and voiceless—the underclasses, women, and ethnic minorities. Melville's aesthetic interest in exploring the limits to our powers of representation corresponds to his political commitment to represent the unrepresentedness, or marginal status, of these social groups.

This book is rooted theoretically in Kant's critical philosophy of representation and theory of the sublime, most importantly his interpretation of the relations between the ethical-political and the aesthetic realms. For Melville, as for Kant, the sublime experience of the limits to our powers of representation is analogous to the experience of freedom and the feeling of respect for ourselves and others. It is a prefiguration of and, in a sense, a prerequisite for democratic, egalitarian relationships. Political theorist Catherine Zuckert has noted the link between Melville's exploration of the limits to our powers of representation and his commitment to democratic thought. According to Zuckert, Melville's work suggests that human beings must "retain their doubts" in order to preserve freedom. She sees Melville exercising "a new kind of democratic intellectual leadership" by demonstrating that democracy requires a "foundation in agnostic toleration" (112, 100). When Melville marks the limits to his own representative powers, he demonstrates respect for the freedom of others and emphasizes the self-determination of his characters and of his readers in the act of interpreting. Like Ishmael faced with the sublime white whale, Melville's readers are free to reflect on the ethical and political implications of their interpretive choices.[3]

Melville's predominant motif for this experience of the limits to our powers of representation, the encounter with the sublime, needs to be distinguished from the nineteenth-century American sublime characterized by Rob Wilson as the Emersonian and Whitmanic sublime of self-aggrandizement and nationalistic euphoria. Melville's sublime is remarkably like Kant's, adamant in its refusal to cross over into and colonize the totality, whether that totality be of the self, nature, or culture. The sublime in Kant and Melville functions in its heterogeneity as a critique of the totalizing thrust of much "sublime" discourse. The Kantian sublime resists closure in its ceaseless vibration, or alternation. Lyotard calls this oscillation "transcendental health"—the "ontological health which is criticism" ("Judiciousness in Dispute," 24–25).

Lyotard's concept of the differend can help us understand how Melville's multiculturalism can be rooted theoretically in Kant's critical philosophy. Combining Kant's notion of the antinomy in the *Critique of Pure Reason* with elements from Wittgenstein, Lyotard defines the differend as "a case of conflict between (at least) two parties, that cannot be equitably resolved for lack of a rule of judgment applicable to both arguments. One side's legitimacy does not imply the other's lack of legitimacy." Kant and Wittgenstein, writes Lyotard, question the terms of "universalist doctrines" that think they can "settle differends (reality, subject, community, finality)." This questioning guards against totalitarianism and lays the groundwork for a "thought of dispersion" (*The Differend,* xi, xiii, xii). This "diaspora" of thought is analogous to the heterogeneous egalitarianism represented in Melville's democratic art. My task is to expose Melville's multiculturalism in this theoretical sense, extending multiculturalism beyond its usual focus on ethnicity to incorporate the categories of class and gender. Kant's philosophy, especially his theory of the sublime, proves a flexible and resilient theoretical tool in the accomplishment of these ends.

Why Kant's theory of the sublime would have such explanatory power as a model for Melville's aesthetic when Melville probably never read a book by Kant is a mystery compounded by the fact that Emerson, who knew German and had read Kant, put this theory to a very un-Kantian use. The question of sources for Melville's aesthetic is an interesting and important one. Although my primary purpose is not to provide a source study, I have addressed the problem of sources in chapter 2. This introductory chapter explores evidence for a Kantian influence on Melville found in the record of the intellectual exchanges between Melville and the German philologist and student of German philosophy George Adler.

Regardless of the immediate sources, the affinities that exist between Melville's and Kant's approaches to the sublime could be rooted in the respect both shared for the Judaic textual tradition linking ethics with a discourse on representation. The commandment "Thou shalt not make to thyself any graven image, nor the likeness of anything which is in heaven or in the earth or under the earth" is cited by Kant as the most sublime passage in the Hebrew scriptures and an example of "the enthusiasm that the Jewish people in their moral period felt for their religion." Kant believed that this strategy of "negative" representation—that is, of marking the limits to our powers of representation in the face of the unrepresentable—"expands the soul" (*Judgment*, 115). Melville apparently concurs when he writes to Hawthorne: "As soon as you say *Me*, a *God*, a *Nature*, so soon you jump off from your stool and hang from the beam. Yes, that word is the hangman. Take God out of the dictionary, and you would have Him in the street" (*Letters*, 125).

In addition to Melville and Kant's sensitivity to the ethical implications of acknowledging the limits to representation, their common concern with the ethical necessity for negotiating a path between the conflicting demands of empiricism and rationalist idealism makes the ties between them even stronger. Melville, like Kant, respected empiricism as a method for understanding the laws of nature and the determining forces in society. At the same time, they both saw in empirical thought a threat to freedom and were committed to preserving a space for self-determination freed from the empirical laws of cause and effect, a space where a new causal chain could be initiated, where change would be possible through the will. The sublime in Kant enacts on an aesthetic level what Susan Meld Shell calls "man's primordial discovery of moral freedom" (68). For Kant and Melville, the sublime serves as a means of experiencing the never-ending conflict between the determinism of empiricism and the individual freedom posited by rationalist idealism.

Melville was no facile liberal hiding behind an ideology of radical individualism and self-reliance. He was deeply aware of the determining economic and political forces that people struggle with every day. The experience of the sublime attests to a self that cannot be reduced to an autonomous, unitary, self-reliant subject; it is always split, vacillating endlessly between two irreconcilable perspectives, the determined and the self-determined. What interests Melville and Kant is the ethical and political importance of the experience of the sublime. By giving us an awareness of our limits *and* our freedom, the sublime can lay the groundwork for a feeling of respect for ourselves and others.

When the quest for the sublime leads to the limits of representation in *Moby-Dick* and *Pierre,* it also leads to the marginal realm of monstrosity. The monstrous whale is not only the subject of *Moby-Dick,* the object of the quest for the sublime, it is also Melville's metaphor for the book itself (see *Letters,* 108, 133). Huge in scale, ill-assorted in parts, *Moby-Dick* and *Pierre* are two of the baggiest monsters in the history of the American novel. This monstrous pair need to be read in the historical context of the "politics of monstrosity," which Christopher Baldick traces in his book *In Frankenstein's Shadow.* The category of the monstrous not only denotes huge scale and ill-assorted parts, but in Melville's day was also associated with "moral aberration" and a rebellious "turning against one's parent" (Baldick, 11, 13). Baldick shows how the category of the "monstrous"—a category often associated with sublime aesthetics—took on political connotations in light of the French Revolution. Burke, whose essay on the sublime did much to bring the monstrous into the realm of art, used the image of the threatening monster with chilling effect as a metaphor for that "monstrous compound"—the new French republic—formed from the parricidal dismemberment of the monarchy and the reassembling of its disjointed parts (Baldick, 18). Radical thinkers like William Godwin, Thomas Paine, and Mary Wollstonecraft were quick to rebut Burke by naming the aristocracy the true monster. Class conflict and the rhetoric of monstrosity fed the mingling of literary and political sensibilities in the Jacobin and gothic novels, including the works of Godwin and Mary Shelley that Melville purchased during his trip to England before writing *Moby-Dick* (Leyda, 351).

Melville's adoption of the rhetoric of monstrosity reflects an anticlassical, antibeautiful thrust to his aesthetic that, in the following passage cited from *Pierre,* implies an anti-aristocratic thrust as well. Melville's metaphor for his monstrous art in *Pierre* is a huge rock "writhing from out the imprisoning earth"—Enceladus the Titan—"scarred and broken," with a "black brow mocked by the upborne moss." This "American Enceladus wrought by the vigorous hand of Nature's self," if compared with that "bold trophy of high art" in the garden of Versailles, will prove to be the "more truthful" of the two (345, 346). As Perry Miller notes, not works of "smoothness and finish, but the spontaneous, even savage" were what the "democratic vision" required of an American literature (95). The spirit of artistic and political rebellion that is represented by Melville's "American Enceladus" and that was celebrated among many of Melville's contemporaries is often read as a reaction against the cultural hegemony of Europe. Although class struggle in the American literary scene often took the form of a "monstrous" rebellion against a classical and aristocratic aesthetic of the beautiful associated with Europe, the aesthetic battle of "taste" over the value of monstrosity was also an American civil war with the battle lines often drawn along political and class affiliations. Many conservatives and reactionaries on the home front objected to the democratic aesthetic of monstrosity (see Miller, 123). In his attempt to democratize his art, Melville attacked the ideology of the literary gentility. His critique of that ideology needs to be understood more in terms of class than national origin, in spite of the nationalistic rhetoric adopted by many of the literary revolutionaries.

Attention to class issues is paramount to understanding Melville's concept of democracy and his call to bring "republican progressiveness into Literature." Careful study of his expressed attitudes toward class is needed. Melville distanced himself from the upper classes, as we see in the following passage from a letter written to Nathaniel Willis: "—tho' there are numbers of fine fellows, and hearts of blood, in the world, whom Providence hath blessed with purses furlongs in length—yet the class of wealthy people are, in the aggregate, such a mob of gilded dunces, that, not to be wealthy carries with it a certain distinction & nobility" (*Letters,* 97). Melville's class consciousness—his hostility toward the upper classes and his valorization of the lower—has escaped the attention of all but a few Melville scholars. H. Bruce Franklin attributes this critical neglect to the class-induced blindness of the academy, an institution dominated by middle- and upper-class interests. My own class consciousness has been shaped by a working-class family and years in the work force before putting myself through college. This experience has sensitized me to Melville's critique of the American class-system's inequalities and injustices.

Perhaps not much has been written about Melville's attitudes toward class because the topic is taboo in our culture. As such, it is subject to a great deal of misunderstanding. In the case of Melville, his class-conscious egalitarianism is sometimes overlooked because of his ex-pressed ambivalence toward the "masses." Melville's attitude expresses the ambivalent social status of the intellectual who still feels ties to the working class. Though Melville was born into a middle-class family with some upper-class connections through his mother and his wife, his class consciousness was undoubtedly shaped by his father's financial ruin and early death and his family's subsequent impoverishment when he was still a boy. Denied the opportunity to go to college, he defiantly declared through the voice of Ishmael, the whale ship, his Harvard and Yale. Melville writes with knowledge of and sympathy for the working class. His experience as a common worker and seaman in his teens and twenties provides abundant grist for his artistic mill and informs the egalitarianism that serves as the political foundation of his aesthetic.

Anyone who wishes to paint a portrait of Melville as a radical egali-tarian democrat has got to come to terms with his ambivalent feel-ings toward the masses. In *White Jacket*, for example, he indulges in an image of the "public" as monstrous in a dialogue between Lemsford and Jack Chase. Lemsford is complaining about the "addle-pated mob and rabble" who failed to appreciate a volume of poems he had published, poems that were "very aggressive on the world":

> "Blast them, Jack, what they call the public is a monster, like the idol we saw in Owhyhee, with the head of a jackass, the body of a baboon, and the tail of a scorpion!"
>
> "I don't like that," said Jack; "when I'm ashore, I myself am part of the public."
>
> "Your pardon, Jack; you are not. You are then a part of the people, just as you are aboard the frigate here. The public is one thing, Jack, and the people another."
>
> "You are right," said Jack; "right as this leg. Virgil, you are a

trump; you are a jewel, my boy. The public and the people! Ay, Ay, my lads, let us hate the one and cleave to the other." (196)

When Melville's beloved Jack Chase objects to Lemsford's monstrous image, Lemsford's distinction between the "public" and the "people" appeses him. Melville makes a similar distinction in a letter to Hawthorne when he avows an "unconditional democracy in all things" while confessing "a dislike to all mankind — in the mass." Melville denies any inconsistency, but defers further discussion calling it an "endless sermon" (*Letters,* 127). Melville apparently needs to assume the stance of hating the public to avoid the risk of playing sycophant to the public tastes and losing sight of his own agenda in an attempt to please. Hating the public may be a survival strategy for Melville, as it was for the poet Lemsford, a way of maintaining his artistic and philosophical integrity in the face of public indifference. Melville did not hate people or popular culture. He just decided to write for what seemed at the time to be an intellectual minority, an "aristocracy of the brain." Although he declares himself "earnest in behalf of political equality," he still admits to accepting the "intellectual estates" (*Letters,* 126).

This "aristocracy of the brain" (*Letters,* 126) is based on talent and merit, not the accident of birth into a particular economic class. It is guaranteed by the "great democratic God" (*Moby-Dick,* 117) who has lifted up persons of such lowly economic status as Bunyon, Cervantes, and Andrew Jackson:

> Thou . . . who didst not refuse to the swart convict, Bunyan, the pale, poetic pearl; Thou who didst clothe with doubly hammered leaves of finest gold, the stumped and paupered arm of old Cervantes; Thou who didst pick up Andrew Jackson from the pebbles; who didst hurl him upon a warhorse; who didst thunder him higher than a throne! Thou who, in all Thy mighty earthly marchings, ever cullest Thy selectest champions from the kingly commons; bear me out in it, O God! (*Moby-Dick,* 117).

With a tone of religious fervor (sidestepping the anthropomorphic with the pronoun *which*), Melville evokes his muse: "thou just Spirit of Equality, which has spread one royal mantle of humanity over all my kind!" (*Moby-Dick,* 117). Melville espouses a "ruthless democracy on all sides" grounded in a political and ethical philosophy that "boldly declares that a thief in jail is as honorable a personage as Gen. George Washington" (*Letters*, 117). In Melville's discourse on human equality, the rhetoric of religion indicates an idealism marking a distinction between the masses as phenomenon and the people as ideal.

In *Moby-Dick* this distinction serves as the basis for a principle governing the author's representations of humanity: "Men may seem detestable as joint stock-companies and nations; knaves, fools, and murderers there may be; men may have mean and meagre faces; but man, in the ideal, is so noble and so sparkling, such a grand and glowing creature, that over any ignominious blemish in him all his fellows should run to throw their costliest robes." Ishmael, with Melville's own sensitivity to class, is quick to point out that the "august dignity" of humanity of which he speaks is not "the dignity of kings and robes, but that abounding dignity which has no robed investiture. Thou shalt see it shining in the arm that wields a pick or drives a spike; that democratic dignity which, on all hands, radiates without end from God; Himself! The great God absolute: The centre and circumference of all democracy! His omnipresence, our divine equality!" This class-conscious, almost mystical, egalitarianism fuels the democratic thrust of Melville's art (*Moby Dick*, 117).

The methodology of this book cannot be reduced to one. The various textual and theoretical problems addressed demand a variety of critical methods. The eclecticism of my approach reflects the eclectic nature of *Moby-Dick* and *Pierre* themselves. This book is not a historical study of the relation of contemporary political events to Melville's texts, although it does bring at least one important political-historical context to light. Nor is it a source study, although it does address theoretically the problem of sources. In order to convey the expansive quality of Melville's political-aesthetic agenda, various artistic, philosophical, cultural, and theoretical contexts will be brought to bear on Melville's texts, contexts generally limited to Melville's historical milieu. They include art history, theories of music, genre study, class culture, theories of the sublime, German philosophy, and gender studies. The book's structure is governed by the underlying symmetry of the diptych form. The connecting thread running throughout is the quest for the sublime and its political-aesthetic implications in Melville's texts. The book ends with a reflection on its origin in my own encounter with Melville's texts as a woman with ties to the working class.

Chapter 2 prepares the reader for the conjunction of Melville's art and Kant's philosophy. Analyzing passages referring to Kant in *Moby-Dick* and *Pierre,* and in the journal Melville kept on his trip to Europe before writing *Moby-Dick,* and evaluating the evidence of a Kantian influence on Melville, the chapter seeks ultimately to problematize the search for sources and influences. Although I hesitate to begin the book with a chapter that may frustrate, as it attempts to answer, empirical yearnings for causal connections, I include it for, among other reasons, Melville's wonderful picture in *Pierre* of the contemporary Kantian scene. Here we find historical precedence for the resistance many Americans feel to German culture and philosophy. The chapter is meant to buffer the criticism of those who think we should stay on American turf when examining the context of Melville's aesthetic and philosophy. Although there are many fine studies of Melville's relation to his American contemporaries, relatively few focus on American-German cultural connections at this time. The relationship between Melville and the German philologist George Adler functions in this chapter as a figure for American-German cultural exchange and as a reminder of the scholarly value of crossing national and interdisciplinary boundaries.

Part I contains three chapters devoted to *Moby-Dick.* They explore the democratic implications of Melville's art by situating the book within the historical context of America's fascination with the sublime and by exploring the affinities between the sublime in Melville and Kant. The main thrust of my reading of *Moby-Dick* is to distinguish two parallel and opposing quests for the white whale: Ahab's fanatic quest to destroy what he determines to be the personification of evil and Ishmael's sublime aesthetic quest to represent the unrepresentable. This device of parallel quests allows us to explore the relations between art and morality, or between representation and the possibility of freedom. Moby Dick, as a sublime object of nature, represents a limit to our powers of representation. As a sublime work of art *Moby-Dick* represents a limit to our powers of interpretation. Melville marks those limits with the oscillating oxymoron, contrasting the oxymoronic strategies of doubling and

multiple perspective with the ultimate stasis implied in the linear teleology of typological interpretation.

The threat to freedom that fanaticism represents in *Moby-Dick* is
contrasted with the threat posed by enthusiasm represented in Melville's next book, *Pierre*. Fanaticism and enthusiasm, according to Kant,
represent modes of thinking our relation to ideas. The transition to
Part 2 on *Pierre* is provided by the distinction between the fanatic and
the enthusiast that Kant draws in the context of the "sublime" Hebrew
law banning representation. The danger of enthusiasm, or unbounded
imagination, arises when the "senses see nothing more before them and
the unmistakable and indelible idea of morality remains" (*Critique of
Judgment*, 115). Pierre's enthusiastic "faith in ye Invisibles" is reflected
in the text's melodramatic rhetoric and its valorization of music as a
nonrepresentational art form (107). Pierre, Lucy, and Isabel function
in the text as aesthetic types of the poetic, musical, and visual arts in
their interrelations. This aesthetic and philosophical context in *Pierre* is
brought into the realm of politics by showing how Melville uses melodrama—its rhetoric of excess, valorization of music, and thematic of
the foreclosed mortgage and landlord-tenant relationship—to critique
the injustices of America's class structure.

Chapter 9 considers evidence that Melville was working under certain gender-determined ideas of genre in forming his literary diptych
Moby-Dick and *Pierre*. In *Pierre* we find Melville shifting generic gears
in an attempt to engage a female readership. A major obstacle for critics
treating Melville's representations of women appears to be class determined. Melville is not so much interested in presenting strong middle-
class female characters like Fanny Fern's "Ruth Hall" triumphing over
adversity in "a man's world," as he is in presenting the unrepresentedness of those who may well be strong but remain oppressed and excluded, like many of the impoverished factory workers and seamstresses
of the working and servant classes. The primary focus of this final chapter is on the title piece for Melville's collection of short stories, "The
Piazza," a brief text that helps us bring together many of the themes
previously discussed. "The Piazza" represents an ending to our journey
circumscribed by Melville himself, in which the narrator's quest for the
sublime meets its limits in a woman's story. Reflecting on my own encounter with Melville's work, I assess the feminist significance of Melville's exploration of the sublime limits to representation.

2

MELVILLE'S KANT

(Being not so much the Portal, as part of the temporary
Scaffold to the Portal of this new Philosophy.)
—PLOTINUS PLINLIMMON, *Pierre, or the Ambiguities*

ALTHOUGH WE HAVE NO RECORD of Melville's ever having read any of
Kant's philosophy, the six scattered references to Kant in *Mardi, Moby-
Dick,* and *Pierre* suggest that Melville had had some exposure to Kant's
thought. We know from the journal that he kept on his trip to England
before writing *Moby-Dick* that during the ocean crossing Melville engaged in long discussions about Kant and German philosophy in general
with a German scholar named George Adler. Although my intention in
placing Melville's work in the context of Kant's theory of the sublime
is not to provide an empirical analysis of Melville's sources, neither is it
to perform a purely ahistorical application. I focus on Melville's philosophical and cultural milieu in general and engage, while problematiz-
ing, the question of sources, much in the spirit of Melville and Kant
themselves. In this sense, I mediate between ahistorical indifference and
the avid historicist's demand for one-to-one correspondences. Although
I do pinpoint some textual sources, in the face of infinite chains linking
historical events I cannot help but feel the dizzying effect of what Hayden White calls the "historical sublime," and I acknowledge the limits
of my scholarly quest (137). Furthermore, my attempt to bracket Mel-

ville's milieu for the sake of history is bound to be contaminated by the present, particularly my interest in contemporary critical issues.

What led me to investigate the relation between Melville and Kant are certain uncanny parallels between their texts, especially their similar formulations of fanaticism and enthusiasm in the context of sublime aesthetics. Kant, in his discourse on the fanatic, has given us a fitting description in philosophical terms of the monomaniacal Ahab who personifies all evil in the sublime white whale. The fanatic, or monomaniac, is incompatible with the sublime because in Kantian terms he collapses the distinction between ideas and empirical phenomena. The experience of the sublime attests to the existence of ideas, which for Kant are outside the causal determinations of empirical thinking. The sublime is a state of mind in which the faculty of Reason, through the idea of totality (an idea that cannot be demonstrated empirically), puts an end to the ceaseless striving of the empirical faculty, Imagination, to represent that which, in terms of power and magnitude, is unrepresentable. Imagination, subjected to Reason's idea of totality in the face of the unrepresentable, feels itself extended into the abyss beyond the limits of sensibility. Beyond sensibility is beyond presentation in any positive sense. The fanatic makes the mistake of thinking that he can represent what is unrepresentable or "will some vision beyond all the bounds of sensibility" (*Critique of Judgment*, 116). By collapsing the two realms of ideas and sensibility, fanatics are led to believe in the representation of moral ideas, like good and evil.

Much depends in the following reading of *Moby-Dick* on this analysis of the incompatibility between fanaticism and the sublime. It accounts for the difference between the book's two parallel quests: Ahab's quest to destroy the white whale and Ishmael's quest to represent it. The reasons for juxtaposing Melville's work with Kant's theory of the sublime become even more compelling when we consider that Kant contrasted the fanatic with another type, the enthusiast (which Melville explored in *Pierre*), and that both types were determined by both writers in the context of sublime aesthetics. This is one sense in which *Moby-Dick* and *Pierre* form a literary diptych: they present contrasting portraits of fanaticism and enthusiasm linked by a common interest in exploring the sublime limits to representation.[1]

Kant's philosophy was widely discussed in Melville's day and apparently achieved a philosophical popularity comparable to existentialism in the 1950s and deconstruction in the 1980s. Melville provides a wonderful glimpse in *Pierre* of the nineteenth-century American Kantian scene when the hero takes up residence in an old church turned office-apartment building, the Church of the Apostles. Here Pierre lives with "mostly artists of various sorts; painters, or sculptors, or indigent students, or teachers of languages, or poets, or fugitive French politicians, or German philosophers." One of his friends, Charlie Millthorpe, even tries to persuade Pierre to "Stump the State on the Kantian Philosophy." The "poor, penniless devils" whom Pierre encounters in the Church of the Apostles "strive to make ample amends for their physical forlornness by resolutely revelling in the region of blissful ideals" (281, 267). The narrator considers their collective philosophy in a passage worth quoting at length. Although playful in tone, it reveals Melville's sincere feelings of respect and gratitude toward his contemporary Kantians. The "mental tendencies" of the "apostles":

> however heterodox at times, are still very fine and spiritual upon the whole; since the vacuity of their exchequers leads them to reject the coarse materialism of Hobbes, and incline to the airy exaltations of the Berkelyan philosophy. Often groping in vain in their pockets, they cannot but give in to the Descartian vortices; while the abundance of leisure in their attics (physical and figurative), unite with the leisure in their stomachs, to fit them in an eminent degree for that undivided attention indispensable to the proper digesting of the sublimated Categories of Kant; especially as Kant (can't) is the one great palpable fact in their pervadingly impalpable lives. These are the glorious paupers, from whom I learn the profoundest mysteries of things; since their very existence in the midst of such a terrible precariousness of the commonest means of support, affords a problem on which many speculative nut-crackers have been vainly employed. Yet let me here offer up three locks of my hair, to the memory of all such glorious paupers who have lived and died in this world. Surely, and truly I honour them—noble men often at bottom—and for that very reason I make bold to be gamesome about them; for where fundamental nobleness is, and fundamental honour is due, merriment is never

accounted irreverent. The fools and pretenders of humanity, and the impostors and baboons among the gods, these only are offended with raillery; since both those gods and men whose titles to eminence are secure, seldom worry themselves about the seditious gossip of old apple-women, and the skylarkings of funny little boys in the street. (267–68)

From Melville's few references to Kant in his texts, it seems that he considered Kant's philosophy and German thought in general to be a continuation of Platonic idealism opposed to materialism. Melville's sole mention of Kant in *Moby-Dick* situates the German philosopher in opposition to the empiricist Locke when Ishmael compares the ship, with the sperm whale's head hanging on one side and the right whale's head hanging on the other, to "some minds" who "forever keep trimming boat" between Locke and Kant. Although Ishmael exhorts the reader, in his characteristic polemic against philosophers, to "throw all these thunderheads overboard" in order to "float light and right," we must note the identification of Kant with the sperm whale, a species that enjoys a privileged status in *Moby-Dick,* a book named after a sperm whale (327; see also Moore, 150). Ishmael dubs the right whale "a Stoic" and the sperm whale "a Platonian who might have taken up Spinoza in his latter years" (335). That Melville associated Kant and all of German thought with Platonic idealism is further suggested in the story of the *Pequod*'s encounter with the only German ship in the book, the *Jungfrau,* or *Virgin.* This ship is devoid of the material commodity, oil, and has never even heard of Moby Dick. When a whale appears, the crew of the *Pequod* (led by Stubb) beat the Germans to the catch and finally leave them in hopeless pursuit of the "uncapturable" fin-back whale, a species that merely resembles the sperm (see chap. 81).

Melville need not have read either Locke or Kant to have been aware of what Merton Sealts has characterized as a raging controversy between the adherents of John Locke's empirical philosophy, which had long been taught in American colleges, and the so-called transcendentalists of New England, who had begun their celebrated revolt against the Lockean position during the 1830s (318). According to Perry Miller, New York represented the stronghold of Locke's no-nonsense empiricism: "There was nothing more characteristic of all New York intellectuals than their instinctive, their spontaneous detestation of the very idea of Germany. And along with it, they could not abide the 'transcendentalism' of New England." This situation was a problem for Melville, who grew up in the New York literary scene but was drawn to that of New England. As Miller writes, "Herman Melville had a mind, but nobody to educate it; on his own he acquired a passion for ideas, and then tried to enter a world where taste was respected, wit admired, erudition praised, but ideas themselves—well, those might turn out to be 'German' and 'transcendental.' If so, they were to be ridiculed and, wherever possible, stamped out" (31).

For examples of Melville's scathing critique of New York materialism we can look to *Pierre* and "Bartleby." The move to New England to write *Moby-Dick* can be read as Melville distancing himself from the constraints of the New York cultural scene and opening himself to the transcendentalism associated with New England and Germany. This is not to suggest that New England transcendentalism, particularly as espoused by Emerson, escaped Melville's critical eye. Melville expresses ambivalent feelings about Emerson. He calls him a "Plato who talks thro' his nose." He criticizes Emerson's arrogance, but he admires "all men who *dive*," and he later became a dedicated student of Emerson's metaphysical poetry (*Letters*, 79). Melville's differences with Emerson can be traced to Emerson's very un-Kantian embrace of the "moral sublime" (see chapter 4).

Merton Sealts characterizes Melville as divided "within his own mind between the claims of experience and reflection, skepticism and intuition, faith and doubt" (319). I suggest that Melville was trying to reconcile the conflicting claims of empiricism and rationalist idealism. With *Moby-Dick*'s conceit of the two whales' heads, Melville may have been declaring his independence from both Locke in New York and Kant in New England. But by situating himself in opposition to both empiricism and a tradition of idealism that he associates with Plato, Melville places himself more in line with Kant's actual philosophy. Kant, like Melville, recognized the value of empiricism and materiality. What Kant himself has to say about Platonic idealism is similar to Melville's characterization in *Moby-Dick* of the Germans in pursuit of the uncapturable fin-back whale. Kant also sought to distance himself from Plato's unlimited extension of reason and in a poetic passage from the *Critique of*

Pure Reason, states his differences with the Greek philosopher, whom he compares to a dove in flight:

> The light dove, cleaving the air in her free flight, and feeling its re-
> sistance, might imagine that its flight would be still easier in empty
> space. It was thus that Plato left the world of the senses, as setting
> too narrow limits to the understanding, and ventured out beyond
> it on the wings of ideas, in the empty space of the pure under-
> standing. He did not observe that with all his efforts he made no
> advance—meeting no resistance that might, as it were, serve as
> a support upon which he could take a stand, to which he could
> apply his powers, and so set his understanding in motion. (47)

Melville seems to have adopted a popular conception of Kant as an idealist. He developed this concept not from careful study of Kant's texts, but from Plato's texts, which, according to Sealts, Melville was reading at this time (281).

Although Melville probably never actually read Kant, at least one place in Melville's writing points to Kant's influence, whether Melville was aware of it or not. In the journal he kept of his trip to Europe before returning to write *Moby-Dick,* Melville writes enthusiastically of his discussions with the German philologist George Adler. It was probably Adler (who shortly after their trip together entered an institution for the mentally ill) whom Melville had in mind when *Pierre's* narrator pays tribute to those "glorious paupers" who taught him the "profoundest mysteries of things." [2] Melville characterizes Adler in his journal as "full of the German metaphysics, & discourse of Kant, Swedenborg, &c." Of one of their talks Melville writes, "We had an extraordinary time & did not break up till after two in the morning. We talked metaphysics continually, & Hegel, Schlegel, Kant &c were discussed under the in-fluence of the whiskey" (*Journal,* 4, 12). Walter Bezanson and Dwight A. Lee have estimated that Melville spent forty-four to forty-five days of his trip with Adler and on at least nine occasions noted German phi-losophy as the main topic of conversation (Bryant, *Companion,* 173–74). Melville and Adler were apparently inseparable from the first night of the voyage. After their second night together, Melville notes some de-tails of their philosophical conversation:

Last evening was very pleasant. Walked the deck with the German, Mr. Adler, till a late hour, talking of "Fixed Fate, Free will, foreknowledge absolute" &c. His philosophy is Coleridgean: he accepts the Scriptures as divine, & yet leaves himself free to inquire into Nature. He does not take it that the Bible is absolutely infallible, & that anything opposed to it in Science must be wrong. He believes that there are things *out* of God and independent of him, — things that would have existed were there no God: — such as that two & two make four; for it is not that God so decrees mathematically, but that in the very nature of things, the fact is thus. (*Journal,* 5)

Although Melville characterized Adler's philosophy as Coleridgean (he had purchased *Biographia Literaria* in 1848, [Leyda, 271]), this summary suggests Adler's familiarity with Kant. As Melville's companion undoubtedly knew, the problem of "foreknowledge absolute," that is, synthetic a priori knowledge, is the central problem of Kant's critical philosophy. Whereas Kant lauded mathematics as a "shining example of how far, independently of experience, we can progress in a priori knowledge," he warned at the same time of the dangers of extrapolating in Platonic fashion from the example of mathematics into the practical realm (*Pure Reason,* 46). Kant was able to critique Platonic idealism because he took empiricism seriously. As a child of the scientific revolution, Kant knew firsthand the power of empiricism's scientific method, but he was deeply concerned about the threat empiricism posed to his cherished metaphysics.

But why would Kant, and Melville, for that matter, cherish metaphysics so? The primary reason lies in the relation of supersensuous ideas to the possibility of freedom. The importance of the theory of the sublime for Kant's philosophy and Melville's art is that the sublime demonstrates on an aesthetic level (that is, prior to cognition) a realm of ideas where freedom from the determinations of nature is thought. Although supersensuous ideas cannot be represented, they can be thought by the Kantian faculty of reason guaranteeing freedom's possibility. To see reason in this positive light is often difficult for us because we tend to associate it with repression, whether in the romantic identification of reason with empirical science, or in the Freudian association of reason with the superego. Since reason in Kant is the faculty responsible for thinking "totality," it can also trigger objections to the act of totalizing in general. I have tried throughout this book to give Kant's texts the careful consideration they deserve. A brief introductory exposition of the basic tenets of Kant's philosophy may be useful to understand the philosophical significance of Melville's encounter with Adler and his artistic quest for the sublime.

The demonstration of the possibility of "foreknowledge absolute" is not only linked to the possibility of self-determination, or individual free will, but also, as Lucian Goldman's reading of Kant demonstrates, linked through Kant's notion of a "common sense" to the idea of community (165, 188). This double focus in Melville and Kant on individual freedom and the relation of the individual to the community accounts for the many parallel motifs in their texts. As we, living under the alienating effects of capitalism, long for community, we must not lose sight of the positive role individualist ideology has played in history, particularly in the middle class's struggle against feudal absolutism. Goldman calls the "individual freedom," which was opened by "trade, the production of commodities for the market, and the individualism which developed from it, . . . one of the most important conquests of the human spirit" (150). Terry Eagleton, in speaking of the way in which the "aesthetic" in Western discourse connotes "self-determination, autonomy, and freedom," warns of the dangers of dismissing these concerns as so much "bourgeois ideology" to be "worsted and ousted by alternative forms of cultural politics. . . . Dialectical thought" should use what it can from this legacy (2, 8). What we can salvage from Kant, according to Goldman, is "the philosophical foundation for the most profound and radical critique" ever made of bourgeois man and society (131, 176).[3]

Before we dive into some technicalities of Kant's thought, however, let us build a bridge through *Biographia Literaria,* the book Melville probably had in mind when he characterized Adler's philosophy as Coleridgean: "Whether any other philosophy be possible but the mechanical; and again, whether the mechanical system can have any claim to be called philosophy; are questions for another place. It is, however, certain, that as long as we deny the former and affirm the latter, we must bewilder ourselves, whenever we would pierce into the *adyta* of causation; and all that laborious conjecture can do, is to fill the gaps of fancy"

(Coleridge, 106–7). This passage introduces empiricism as a "mechanical" system built according to the deterministic law of natural causality and also characterizes the "stand off" between empiricism and speculative metaphysics that Kant attempted to mediate in order to preserve the possibility of freedom. Particularly striking in this passage is Coleridge's image of piercing into the "*adyta* of causation," an image Melville may have had in mind when he wrote Ahab's "pasteboard mask" speech. In this context, Ahab's quest can be interpreted as a search for a first or final cause in a deterministic world of cause and effect.

The conflict Melville touches on in his journal entry between empiricism and metaphysics Kant attempts to resolve in his *Critique of Practical Reason* by first considering the empiricist's claim that all knowledge comes from experience. He accuses Hume, for example, of not properly understanding the true "synthetic a priori" nature of mathematical propositions. They did not proceed analytically, as Hume had claimed, from the principle of identity. Furthermore, if knowledge was determined by objects, then, Kant argued, synthetic a priori knowledge, like mathematical propositions, would be impossible. In order to demonstrate the possibility of such knowledge independent from experience, Kant needed to examine the role of reason. He showed that the unlimited extension of speculative reason eventually leads to antinomies, pairs of mutually contradicting propositions. The problem with reason, according to Kant, is that it can prove too much that cannot be contradicted by experience. This leaves it vulnerable to attacks from empiricists who consider the results of reason to be simply meaningless, empty speculation. Kant responds to their criticism by examining the contradictory claims of the antinomy between the concept of natural causality, on the one hand, which requires the connection of events under the law of empirical science to be the only connection, and the concept of freedom, on the other, which requires that a new causal chain be initiated by an act of will that is not the effect of any earlier event. In order to solve this antinomy, Kant posits a distinction between appearances and things-in-themselves, between phenomena, which can be known, but only as conditioned by our sense of time and space, and noumena, which are unconditioned. Noumena, or things-in-themselves, can be thought, but not known, and can only be negatively represented. Kant then reveals the two contradictory positions of the antinomy to be both true depending on whether one is dealing with appearances in the first case or with the relation of appearances to things-in-themselves in the second.

With his distinction between phenomena and noumena, Kant breaks the dogmatic hold of empiricism. Kant recognized a threat to freedom, not only in the mechanical conception of causality, but also in the skeptical position of empiricists like Hume who believed causality to be an illusion. Causality is only an illusion, writes Kant, in reference to things-in-themselves. Hume makes the mistake of taking objects of experience for things-in-themselves. By denying reason, Hume replaces the possibility of freedom with "blind chance." The concept of freedom is, according to Kant, "the stumbling block of all empiricists, but the key to the most sublime practical principle for critical moralists, who see through it, that they must proceed rationally." Whereas, in the critique of pure reason, freedom is merely a possibility and a necessity to keep speculative reason from contradicting itself, it is a "fact" in the application of reason to the practical realm. The fact of freedom is given for Kant by the moral law and points to the existence of the intelligible world of ideas. In fact, according to Kant, the concept of freedom is finally the only thing that can be known of the intelligible or supersensuous world (*Practical Reason*, 54, 53, 8, 44, 73).

Kant claimed in his preface to the first critique to be limiting knowledge to make room for faith. At the limit of knowledge, Kant bridges the gap between the phenomena and the noumena with the supersensible and inscrutable concept of freedom. We emerge as creatures of two different worlds. As phenomena, we are subject to laws of natural necessity. But each person, writes Kant, is also "conscious of his own existence as thing-in-itself" and "views his existence so far as it does not stand under temporal conditions," but "is determinable by laws which he gives to himself through reason" (*Practical Reason*, 90, 101). The noumena present to thought the identity of determined subject and self-determining author. Herein lies the great Kantian revolution in which "finality no longer has a theological principle, but rather, theology has a 'final' human foundation" (Deleuze, 68). For Lucian Goldman, the concept of God in Kant's "Copernican revolution" becomes "no more than the theological expression of man's aspiration towards a perfect community" (91).

On the basis of Melville's reference to Kantian "subjectivism" in *Pierre* (409), Merton Sealts speculates that Melville may have had Kant's philosophy in mind when he wrote the doubloon chapter in *Moby-Dick* (324). The journal entry above provides some evidence for the Kantian influence we see in Melville's art. The first thing that strikes me about Melville's transcription of the Miltonic phrase, "Fixed Fate, Free will, and foreknowledge absolute," is Melville's decreasing use of capitals. I detect a descent from the dogmatic world of Calvinist theology, that is Fixed Fate, to the secular world of foreknowledge absolute, with Free will acting as the mediating link. In contrast to Kant, whose approach to the problem of freedom begins from the perspective of mathematics (that is, foreknowledge absolute), Melville begins with Calvinist dogma (Fixed Fate). The notion of divinity that emerges in Melville's passage, however, is not an all-determining being, but a text: Adler "accepts the scripture as divine" — and presumably Melville concurs. Several months later, Melville performs a similar move when he characterizes Shakespeare as "divine," comparing him to Jesus and predicting that "if another Messiah ever comes twill be in Shakesper's person" (*Letters,* 77).

The term *Divinity* signifies here a kind of textual truth that Melville, summarizing Adler, juxtaposes with the truth claims of another "text," science — without denying the validity of either. Their contradictory claims to truth are reconciled by positing the existence of things outside God's determining power: "things out of God and independent of him, — things that would have existed were there no God," as, for example, mathematical propositions. Most importantly for Melville, in this gap opened by "foreknowledge absolute," appears the possibility of "free will" in opposition to "Fixed Fate." Adler's exposition of the basics of Kant's philosophy seems to have opened a realm of possibilities for Melville, which he explores in depth in his next major writing project, *Moby-Dick.*

PART I
Reading *Moby-Dick*

3

ARTIST OF THE
SUBLIME

Give me a condor's quill! Give me Vesuvius' crater for an inkstand! Friends,
hold my arms! For in the mere act of penning my thoughts of this Leviathan,
they weary me, and make me faint with their outreaching, comprehensiveness
of sweep, as if to include the whole circle of the sciences, and all the generations
of whales, and men, and mastodons, past, present, and to come, with all the
revolving panoramas of empire on earth, and throughout the whole universe,
not excluding its suburbs.

—*Moby-Dick,* CHAP. 104

AT A TIME WHEN the European aesthetic was beginning to shift from
romanticism to realism, many American artists persisted in working
within the "romantic" tradition of the sublime.[1] Perry Miller notes the
centrality of the quest for the sublime in Melville's day, particularly
in the aspirations of the literary-political Young America movement—
the world "into which *Moby-Dick* breached" (297). In order to understand the intensity with which the American artistic community took
up the quest for the sublime, we need to see at the heart of this quest
a reflection on the relations between art and the ideals of democracy.
There are as many different interpretations of this relationship as there
are political perspectives. The quest for the sublime in American art is
not a simple ideological phenomenon. A variety of voices can be distinguished as artists competed with each other to represent the sublime.
Moby-Dick was Melville's entry into the national competition. His re-

lation to the quest for the sublime is a complex one. John Higham has called Melville America's chief "critic and practitioner of boundlessness" (4). Within *Moby-Dick* are contained many of the interpretive conflicts surrounding the meaning of the sublime for Melville's contemporaries.

In Ishmael's treatment of the two sacred icons of the sublime in American art at this time, George Washington and Niagara Falls, we find an indication of Melville's typically irreverent ambivalence. Ishmael substitutes the Polynesian native Queequeg for the figure of Washington. There was something "sublime" about Queequeg, he seemed "always equal to himself." "Phrenologically" speaking, the shape of Queequeg's head, especially the forehead, reminds Ishmael of the popular busts of Washington. "Queequeg," he concludes, "was George Washington cannibalistically developed" (50).[2]

Ishmael puts a similar twist on another popular icon of the natural sublime when he evokes Niagara Falls in the book's opening meditation on water. This paragraph, of which the image of the falls forms a crux, begins with a "picturesque" landscape artist who needs to incorporate a stream into his painting in order to achieve the desired dreamy effect. Ishmael then moves quickly through the vast "Prairies" where one will find one "charm wanting. . . . Water—there is not a drop of water there!" After the first mention of water, Ishmael asks, "Were Niagara but a cataract of sand would you travel your thousand miles to see it?" Ishmael follows this substitution of sand for the waters of Niagara with a series of tension-building questions about water's fascination. The paragraph ends with the story of Narcissus as the "key to it all" (5). The force of Ishmael's rhetoric, in this case his use of the falls as a reversal initiating a peroration, breaks the reader's attachment to the image or icon and displaces its centrality to reveal the idea behind and, in a sense, independent of the sensible image.[3] That Ishmael would offer, at this point, the story of Narcissus as "the key" suggests that the attachment to the image—or, in Kantian terms, the inability or refusal to distinguish phenomena from noumena—is at the root of Narcissus's self-destruction.

Ishmael's seemingly irreverent iconoclasm is actually an act of piety in Melville's version of the sublime. Ishmael's commitment to holding the line and refusing to cross over into the "transcendent" has ethical implications. The problem of "crossing over"—of representing that which, in Kantian terms, is beyond representation—forms the crux of much critical controversy in Melville's time over the significance of the sublime and its relation to democratic values.[4] Many saw a moral threat in the indeterminacy that results from acknowledging limits to one's representative powers. In the face of the atheistic implications of Burke's horrific sublime, for example, some called for an American sublime more befitting the goals and ideals of a "Christian" republic. This American version of the sublime would harness the passions released by the sublime object of nature in the service of morality (Sanford, 142–43). The moral sublime was more congenial to those who interpreted the vast continent as a call from God to establish his kingdom on earth in the spirit of manifest destiny.

In *Moby-Dick* Melville presents these two interpretations of the sublime—the Burkean horrific and the Christian moral—in the images of two contrasting paintings of the sublime in nature.[5] The first painting illustrates qualities associated with Burke's sublime, such as darkness, obscurity, and the representation of overwhelming natural power dwarfing human existence. It hangs in a secular setting, the entry to the Spouter Inn. It is a "boggy, soggy squitchy picture enough to drive a nervous man distracted." Yet "there is a sort of indefinite, half-attained, unimaginable sublimity about it. . . ." It consists of such "unaccountable masses of shades and shadows that at first you almost thought some ambitious young artist, in the time of the New England hags, had endeavored to delineate chaos bewitched. But by dint of much and earnest contemplation, and oft-repeated ponderings, and especially by throwing open the little window towards the back of the entry, you at last come to the conclusion that such an idea, however wild, might not be altogether unwarranted" (12).

After much deliberation, Ishmael finally determines the painting to represent a foundering ship during a hurricane off Cape Horn on whose masts a giant whale is about to impale itself. Burke's empirical theory of the sublime focuses on the terrible, chaotic meaninglessness of nature's sublime power. The unredeemable horror of the Spouter Inn painting is contrasted with the representation of Christian grace found in the painting hanging in the whaleman's chapel. In this painting the power of nature is superseded by a transcendent order. Again we have a picture of a ship beating against a terrible storm, but floating in the sky above in a little island of light is an "angel's face," which seemed to say "beat on,

beat on, thou noble ship, and bear a hardy helm; for lo! the sun is breaking through; the clouds are rolling off—serenest azure is at hand" (40).

Melville mediates between these two versions of the sublime in *Moby-
Dick* in the same way he mediates between the claims of empiricism and
rationalist idealism. Although Melville has traditionally been associated
with the darkness of the Burkean sublime, he deviates from Burke in
his interest in the moral implications of the experience of the sublime,
especially as those implications impinge upon democratic values. In this
sense Melville's sublime is more like Kant's. Although Melville's sublime
is not to be confused with the moral sublime's positive representation
of the transcendent, neither is his iconoclastic rejection of the moral
sublime an embrace of utter nihilism.[6]

These rather complex philosophical and aesthetic problems are structurally laid out in *Moby-Dick* in the contrast between Ishmael's quest
to represent the whale and Ahab's quest to destroy it. Ishmael functions
as the artist of the sublime as he attempts to represent the unrepresentable. Ahab is the fanatic who tries to destroy the sublime. The dual
structure of parallel quests reveals affinities and disjunctures between
Ishmael's and Ahab's quests. Imagery of the hunt, for example, links the
two quests and, in Ishmael's case, reveals the limits of the epistemologi-
cal quest to know/conquer the whale as an object of knowledge. Most
importantly for our purposes, the device of double quests in the book
allows for reflection on the responsibilities of a socially conscious art or
artist in a democratic society. *Moby-Dick* represents one artist's response
to the problems we face in our society as we strive for greater democratization.

To establish Ishmael as an artist of the sublime is to invite comparisons between Ishmael and Melville. One of the biggest temptations
among Melville critics has been to conflate the first-person narrator of
Moby-Dick with the author. It is easy to understand why we do this
when we consider that Ishmael and Melville are both writing the same
book. One can even find a point of convergence in the text between the
two "authors" when Ishmael/Melville inscribes the moment of writing
in chapter 85 as "fifteen and a quarter minutes past one o'clock P.M. of
this sixteenth day of December, A.D. 1850" (370). Ishmael articulates the
writer's task in the book, which consists partly of finding some mode to
represent the sublime Moby Dick. *Moby-Dick* has a dual plot structure.

The story of Ahab's quest has achieved mythic status. It is so intense and mesmerizing, it cannot help but dominate our perception of the book. The story of Ishmael's quest is equally important, however, and should not be overlooked. While Ishmael is writing the history of Ahab's quest to capture the whale, he is also attempting to capture the whale in words and reflecting on the development of his own life in the process. A reading of this other, relatively neglected, plot not only establishes the role of Ishmael as artist of the sublime but also reveals a shape, or narrative logic, to the cetological sections of the book. Ishmael's quest to capture the whale is a progressive study in the methodology of representation, including critical methodologies for representing texts. In the chapter titled "Cetology" the whales appear as books. Ishmael's quest, in this sense, becomes an allegory of reading—a reflection on the methodology of reading this book named for the sublime white whale and of reading the sublime in general. The plot of Ishmael's quest functions as a subtle critique of the politics of Ahab's quest and offers a method for interpreting the significance of the *Pequod*'s destruction.

The following plot analysis of Ishmael's quest to represent the whale consists of two parts. It begins with the autobiography of Ishmael, which in its structure recalls the *Künstlerroman*, a novelistic genre tracing the early development of the artist. Ishmael's *Künstlerroman* ends with the opening line of *Moby-Dick*, "Call me Ishmael." The second part of the analysis reveals the cetological plot of Ishmael's artistic quest to represent the whale in the writing of his book.

The story of Ishmael's life, when its chronology is extracted from the text, represents the autobiography of the author, in which the event narrated at the end of the book—the destruction of the *Pequod*—functions as the major turning point in his artistic development. Though Ishmael does not become an artist until he is compelled (like Job's anonymous messenger) to tell of his near escape from total destruction, we can recognize the development of his "artistic" inclinations in his earlier days. In a rather conventionally romantic representation of the artist, the youthful Ishmael appears curious and eager for adventure, but also dreamy, retrospective, and alienated from his surroundings. In the single glimpse he gives of his early childhood, Ishmael tells of being punished by his stepmother for climbing up the chimney in imitation of the chimney sweep. Sent to his bed while it is still light out, the imaginative child has frightening visions of death. Ishmael's alienation is clear in the opening sections of the book when he desires to break away from those on shore and characterizes the bond he forms with Queequeg as exceptional.

While on board ship, Ishmael seems more inclined toward the intellectual and contemplative life than the utilitarian business of whaling. Ishmael may have sworn "oaths of violence and revenge" along with the other members of the crew after Ahab's stirring speech (179), but his actions while on board the ship suggest that he lacks devotion to the hunt. When he does appear on the stage of the ship, it is usually alone or with Queequeg, in moments of lyrical meditation that prefigure his future solitary hours as a writer. His reflections stand in sharp contrast to the frenzied movement of Ahab's plot to destroy the white whale. When he is looking out from the masthead, for example, whales are "as scarce as hen's teeth" (159). Ishmael has the power to bring the chase to a halt because, lost in thought, he neglects to look out for whales. In "The Tryworks" he nearly capsizes the ship when he loses himself to night visions while at the helm. Ishmael's reflective moments aboard ship are often interrupted by the utilitarian business of whaling. The philosophical Loom of Time metaphor that he constructs while weaving a mat with Queequeg, for example, is brought to an abrupt close by Tashtego's call from the masthead on sighting the first whale of the voyage.

Ishmael undergoes two major changes in the book. Many have noted the turning point in Ishmael's life when he meets Queequeg and says, "No more my splinted heart and maddened hand were turned against the wolfish world. This soothing savage had redeemed it" (51). Ishmael's love for Queequeg has a profound effect on his moral and aesthetic development. Equally important, however, is the change Ishmael undergoes after the destruction of the *Pequod*. He himself distinguishes two selves, a before and after, in the chapter given the same name as the book, "Moby Dick." For several preceding chapters, Ishmael drops out of the narrative and virtually fuses his identity with the crew as his previously continuous first-person narration is erased and replaced with a series of dramatic monologues. This dramatic sequence climaxes in the "Midnight, Forecastle," which ends with the voice of Pip. The subsequent chapter, "Moby-Dick," marks Ishmael's return to the role of first-person narrator with a confession, "I, Ishmael, was one of that crew. . . .

Ahab's quenchless feud seemed mine" (179). With this confession, Ishmael, as the only survivor of the shipwreck, distances himself from the person he once was.

When on board the *Pequod*, Ishmael is easily taken in, his identity subordinated, even subsumed by Ahab's quest. But in the act of writing he subsumes Ahab's quest within the parameters of his book as he takes on the triple task of telling the story of his own life (including his relationship with Queequeg), telling the story of Ahab's quest, and representing as fully as possible the object of that quest, the white whale, an object that does not make its actual appearance until the last few pages of the book.

Ishmael's task of representing the whale takes on the proportions of Ahab's quest, creating a tension in the book between the dynamic quality of Ahab's chase and the relatively static quality of Ishmael's attempts to capture in words the object of that chase. Within Ahab's drama itself, Ishmael is a minor, undistinguished, and unnamed character—simply one of the anonymous crew united behind the captain. Rarely does he interact with any of the main characters in Ahab's drama, except Queequeg. The story of the friendship that develops between Ishmael and Queequeg forms an alternative plot to the story of Ahab's quest for Moby Dick's destruction.

In the interim between the *Pequod*'s sinking and the writing of the book, Ishmael emerges in acts more closely related to his future role as a writer. First he appears as the teller of the *Town Ho*'s tale. When Ishmael's Chilean listeners require him to swear on a Bible to verify the truth of his story, we are reminded of the history of Melville's own writing career when he was challenged to attest to the veracity of his first two books, *Typee* and *Omoo*. "*Town Ho*'s Story" is, chronologically speaking, prior to the writing of *Moby Dick* for Ishmael, and its characterization of Moby Dick as an instrument of divine retribution may suggest a moral interpretation of the white whale (the moral sublime) that is superseded by the more ambiguous presentation we ultimately get in the book as a whole.

"*Town Ho*'s Story" presumably grew out of Ishmael's experience on the *Pequod*. Ishmael's next appearance in the chronology of his life is in the act of collecting "research" on the whale during a journey to the Bower in the Arsacides. Here he measures the skeleton of a stranded whale, now the site of a native temple. In this sacred space and in the presence of the island's priests, Ishmael undergoes a rite of initiation into his future role of writer that parallels Ahab's ritual initiation of the crew in the hunt for the white whale. In what can be read as a comment on the contemporary critical controversies over the significance of the sublime, Melville represents a group of priests arguing vehemently among themselves in response to Ishmael's question concerning the size of the whale. While the priests are thus occupied, Ishmael measures the whale himself and has the numbers cut into the skin of his "right arm" (his writer's arm), so as not to forget them. He does not trouble himself "with the odd inches" because he is "crowded for space," and wishes the "untatooed parts" of his body "to remain a blank page for a poem" he was "composing" (451). Ishmael is now ready to begin his book and appears next in the act of writing the opening line, "Call me Ishmael."

Ishmael's development as an artist leads directly to his artistic quest to represent the whale in words. I read the episodes in Ishmael's artistic quest in the order they appear in the text *without* regard this time to their suggested chronology, even though the episodes sometimes overlap with the autobiographical sections. The plot of Ishmael's quest read according to the book's sequence takes on a shape and narrative logic of its own. Though the quest centers around the representations of the whale, I prefer to think of it in narrative terms in order to stress its teleological, plotlike structure in contrast to the way it is usually considered as a "cetological center." This narrative of Ishmael's aesthetic quest for the sublime is interwoven throughout the text with the narrative of Ahab's quest, as if Ishmael is compelled to relive the trauma of Ahab's quest, to repeat it this time on an aesthetic level in order to gain some control over the previous trauma through the act of writing. Most importantly the parallel structure allows for a study of the affinities and contrasts between Ahab's and Ishmael's methods of approaching the sublime.

The story of Ishmael's quest to represent the whale follows specific representations of the whale as they appear successively in the text, beginning with the act of naming the book *Moby-Dick; or, The Whale*, an act that transforms the book into a talisman for evoking the whale in all its bulky presence. From the opening epigraph in which the whale is presented as a "moving land" who "spouts out a sea," it appears that this task of calling up the whale is not going to be an easy one. The search for a stable point of view, a ground from which to observe this "moving land" that surrounds itself with a sea, must be abandoned. Before casting off from land, however, Ishmael offers definitions and contexts from a landlocked perspective: first, in the contradictory etymology of the word *whale;* second, in the translations of the word *whale* provided by the "consumptive usher to a grammar"; and finally in the "bird's eye view" consisting of extracts gleaned from the "Vatican and street-stalls of the earth" (xvii). These situate the whale in a linguistic and literary context, providing a transition from the sea to the page.

When Ishmael appears in the book's first chapter, it is in movement toward the sea motivated primarily by the "overwhelming idea of the great whale himself." This idea gives way to a dreamlike image, or "conceit" as Ishmael calls it: "two and two there floated into my inmost soul, endless processions of the whale, and, midmost of them all, one grand hooded phantom, like a snow hill in the air." The fact that Ishmael's vision of the white whale occurs before he ever hears of Moby Dick can indicate a form of knowledge independent from experience, arising in this case, it seems, from the desire to transcend the bipolar structure of thought and language itself. Ishmael then moves from this "conceit" to consider the representation of the whale in the Spouter Inn's painting as an image of the horrific sublime. The whale makes its next appearance at the chapel when Father Mapple interprets Jonah's whale as an agent of God's will. After contrasting the horrific and the moral interpretations of the sublime whale, Ishmael then launches into his scientific examination of the whale in the cetology chapter. Before he begins his scientific investigation, however, he must settle on a definition of the whale, which he takes from Jonah in the Bible: the whale is a spouting fish with a horizontal tale. Ishmael's recourse to this sacred text resolves the irresolvable controversy over the whale's definition and provides the ground on which Ishmael can take his first step in his empirical "classification of the constituents of a chaos," that is, the sorting of whales by genus and species (7, 134).

With Ahab's introduction of Moby Dick to the crew, Ishmael's quest takes on an additional dimension. The quest to represent the *white* whale, the specific object of Ahab's quest, forms an all-important subplot within the plot of Ishmael's quest to represent whales in general and parallels the movement of Ahab's chase. When Ahab bestows a name on Ishmael's "grand hooded phantom," this quest for the white whale properly begins. It is at this moment that Ishmael fuses with the crew and gives over the text to the ship's many voices. After this dramatic interlude Ishmael's voice returns. He contemplates the legends that have grown up around the white whale and reflects on the difference between his and Ahab's interpretations of the white whale. For Ahab, Moby Dick is "all evil . . . visibly personified" (184). Ahab's moral determination of the white whale contrasts with Ishmael's aesthetic one. It is the indeterminacy of its color, the whiteness of the whale, that intrigues Ishmael.

After these crucial distinctions are made, Ishmael suggests that the white whale has visited the ship in ghostly form as the "spirit spout." From now until Moby Dick's appearance "in the flesh" in the final chapters of the book, the white whale is only represented through the various interpretations presented in the tales collected from the gams. The storytellers' representations of Moby Dick form another subplot in Ishmael's quest to represent the whale, one that properly begins with Ahab's exposition of the white whale in "The Quarter-Deck" and ends with Ishmael's own story of the *Pequod*'s fate. Of the eight ships encountered in the gams, only the *Virgin (Jungfrau)* from Germany, the *Rosebud* from France, and the *Bachelor* from New Bedford say they have had no contact with Moby Dick and have never even heard of him. The names and nationalities of the ships encountered in the gams suggest a philosophical allegory. Neither the American *Bachelor* nor the German *Virgin* have encountered Moby Dick. Perhaps the *Bachelor* represents an excessive hedonistic materialism and the German *Virgin* a dematerialized purity, both of which would preclude the experience of the sublime. The same could be said of the excessive refinement and decadence exhibited by the French *Rosebud*. The first ship to have some experience with Moby Dick is the *Town Ho*. In the *Town Ho*'s story, the white whale appears to dispense justice by killing Radney. The next tale we hear of Moby Dick is told by Gabriel of the *Jeroboam*, who sees Moby Dick as the Shaker God incarnate. In both of these gams, Moby Dick is determined as a force in the service of some higher moral order.

Although Moby Dick is not explicitly represented in "The Doubloon," his presence is evoked by what the crew consider to be the white whale's "talisman," the gold doubloon. This chapter forms a nodal point in Ishmael's quest to represent Moby Dick, after which the act of interpreting the stories of Moby Dick becomes more and more problematic. The subsequent gam with the English ship, the *Samuel Enderby*, strains our powers of perception as we try in vain to distinguish lies from truth in the stories of Boomer and Bunger.[7] There is little doubt, however, that Moby Dick left his mark on the captain of the *Enderby*, apparently while it was in the incredible act of freeing a group of whales from some whaler's lines. The crew of the American *Bachelor* has never heard of Moby Dick, but the captain-father on the American ship, the *Rachel*, loses his two sons to the white whale. As Captain Gardiner flounders in Moby Dick's murderous wake, his Christian appeal to Ahab falls on deaf ears. In the last story told through the device of the gam, the *Delight* tells a mournful tale of five dead.

Ishmael returns to a consideration of whales in general after the first gam with the *Town Ho* by examining various visual representations of whales through the years: whales "in Paint; in Teeth; in Wood; in Sheet-Iron; in Stone; in Mountains; in Stars" (269). Ishmael then moves beyond the abstraction of the cetological system and the artistic representations of whales in word and image, and discusses the whale's diet as if to bait the hook for the first catch of the voyage. When the first whale is caught, Ishmael begins cutting into the surface of the whale, removing the skin and dissecting the heads of a sperm whale and a right whale for a comparative anatomical study. It is the sperm whale's head that most intrigues Ishmael and he devotes several chapters to it.

In the chapter titled "The Prairie" Ishmael tries to read the head as a "Physiognomist or Phrenologist." "Perhaps the most imposing physiognomical view to be had of the Sperm Whale," he writes, "is that of the full front of his head. This aspect is sublime." The whale has no nose. Its eyes are on opposite sides of its head. All one sees from the frontal view is a massive wall-like brow: "this high and mighty god-like dignity inherent in the brow is so immensely amplified, that gazing on it, in that full front view, you feel the Deity and the dread powers more forcibly than in beholding any other object in living nature. For you see no one point precisely; not one distinct feature is revealed; no nose, eyes, ears or mouth; no face; he has none proper; nothing but that one broad firmament of a forehead, pleated with riddles." Physiognomically speaking, Ishmael concludes, the sperm whale is a "sphinx." Ishmael merely puts its "brow before you" for you to read if you can. After considering the whale's brain, Ishmael returns to the spout and the tail, the attributes by which the whale was identified according to Ishmael's definition. Ishmael then places the whale in its element and observes its social life and means of propagation, thereby completing his representation of the whale from a zoological perspective (346, 347).

Ishmael next considers the whale's value as a commodity (oil and ambergris) and the sign of our appropriation of that value: the whale's castrated and skinned penis. This section concludes with the burning of the whale oil, the source of light energy in man's battle against the darkness. In "The Doubloon" the notion of value and light energy (the doubloon as analogous to the sun) is explored in relation to the structure of quests in general. The doubloon, the locus of value on the ship, is redeemable by the first person to sight the white whale. As a symbol of the desired presence of the absent whale, the doubloon represents symbolic structure in general. This structure of absence and presence is reproduced in the next episode of Ishmael's quest to represent the whale, when Ishmael measures the skeleton of a dead whale and tatoos the numbers on his body. In Ishmael's last discourse on the whale, before Moby Dick makes his entrance, he considers the whale's existence in time. Ishmael concludes that since time began with man and ancient fossils demonstrate that the whale existed before man, then the whale can be said to have existed before time, and, Ishmael predicts, the whale will exist beyond man's time into eternity. For the remainder of the book, Ahab's drama takes center stage with the grand finale consisting of the appearance and escape of Moby Dick.

Ishmael's quest, as I have determined it, is primarily a representational one, distinguished from Ahab's quest to destroy the whale. There is, however, an important link between the two quests on the level of textual imagery. In the chapter titled "Cetology" Ishmael draws on the tools of the hunt, the harpoon and the whale line, to characterize the act of representing the whale in its "broad genera" in terms similar to Ahab's quest to destroy the whale by "cutting in" and connecting lines: "To grope down into the bottom of the sea after them; to have one's hands among the unspeakable foundations, ribs, and very pelvis of the world; this is a fearful thing. What am I that I should essay to hook the nose of this leviathan! The awful tauntings in Job might well appal me.

'Will he (the leviathan) make a covenant with thee?' Behold the hope of him is vain!' " (136). In Job God taunts those who would hope to gain sovereignty over the leviathan: "Canst thou draw out leviathan with a hook? or his tongue with a cord which thou lettest down?" (Job 41:1).[8] The biblical text's imagery of the hook and line suggests the notion of a covenant. Fastening to the leviathan, cutting into its flesh and attaching a line, is read by Ishmael as a mark of the covenant. Drawing on this biblical imagery, Ishmael links the representational task of conceptualizing the whale into assorted forms, with the attempt to capture and dominate the leviathan by means of a covenant. This act of subordination, in turn, becomes a figure for the quest for a kind of knowledge that is unavailable. The leviathan, according to God, is "a king over all the children of pride" (Job 41:34). Hunting for the whale entails the threat of death or dismemberment. To fasten to the whale, one has to enter his vicinity, meet him face to face in his own element; but in the words of Job "who can discover the face of his garment?" (Job 41:13). The old sailor begging on the London docks is one witness to the whale's destructive power. This sailor speaks not a word, but holds a "painted board before him, representing the tragic scene in which he lost his leg." The "incredulous world" should believe him, cries Ishmael, fellow survivor of another whaling disaster. The three whales painted in the beggar's picture "are as good whales as were ever published in Wapping, at any rate" (269). The painter himself paid a dear price for them.

After considering numerous representations of the whale, some "monstrous" and some "less erroneous" pictures and various representations of the whale in paint, teeth, wood, sheet-iron, stone, mountains, and stars, Ishmael concludes that "the great Leviathan is that one creature in the world which must remain unpainted to the last. . . . So there is no earthly way of finding out precisely what the whale really looks like. And the only mode in which you can derive even a tolerable idea of his living contour, is by going a whaling yourself; but by so doing, you run no small risk of being eternally stove and sunk by him. Wherefore, it seems to me you had best not be too fastidious in your curiosity touching this Leviathan" (264). Yet who is more fastidious in matters touching the whale than Ishmael himself? The book stands as a testament to his insatiable desire to know everything about it and to communicate this knowledge to others. He categorizes whales; he considers various representations of them in word and image; he captures them, cuts into them, dissects and even eats them.

There is a limit, however, to his powers of representation. Take, for example, the whale's tail, of which Ishmael carefully isolates five types of movement: "First, when used as a fin for progression; Second, when used as a mace in battle; Third, in sweeping; Fourth, in lobtailing; Fifth, in peaking flukes." His detailed description of each movement ends with the peaking of the flukes, which, "excepting the sublime *breach* [is] perhaps the grandest sight to be seen in all animated nature." Ishmael then moves from the sublime to the ridiculous by comparing the whale with the puny elephant (a comparison that he carries into a footnote). When he returns to the body of the text, he speaks of tail movements that seem to be gestures, but "remain wholly inexplicable," along with "other motions of the whale in his general body," that are "full of strangeness, and unaccountable to his most experienced assailant." He concludes: "Dissect him how I may, then, I but go skin deep; I know him not, and never will. But if I know not even the tail of this whale, how understand his head? much more, how comprehend his face, when face he has none? Thou shall see my back parts, my tail, he seems to say, but my face shall not be seen. But I cannot completely make out his back parts; and hint what he will about his face, I say again he has no face" (376, 378, 379).

In attempting to capture the movements of the whale's tail Ishmael reaches a limit to his powers of representation as when he encounters the "face," which is not properly speaking a face at all, having "no one point precisely" on which to focus, "no nose, eyes, ears or mouth" (346). Confronted with this "sublime aspect" of the whale, Ishmael has textual recourse to the encounter between Moses and his god, in which Moses asks God to "shew me now thy way." It was in Exodus that God first revealed his proper name, Jehovah. But even though God is said to speak to Moses "face to face," when Moses asks to see God's face, God refuses, stating "there shall no man see me and live" (Exod. 33:13, 6:2, 33:11, 33:20). Instead of showing his face, God shows the palm of his hand (along with his "tail"). The face of the whale is like the blank palm of the hand, except that the whale, in contrast to Moses' god, is not *hiding* his face because the whale's face is "no face." The word *face* indicates some thing in reference to the whale, but the pointing gesture is blocked by the opposing gesture of the raised palm.[9]

Ishmael is drawing from a long tradition in sublime aesthetics when, faced with his failure to represent the whale in its totality, he has recourse to the Hebrew rhetoric of sublimity. The book of Exodus contains what Kant considered to be the most sublime statement in the Hebrew scriptures, that is, the ban on representation as the condition of God's covenant with Moses' people: "Thou shalt not make unto thee any graven image, or any likeness of anything that is in heaven above, or that is in the earth beneath, or that is in the water under the earth" (Exod. 20:4). The first theorist of the sublime, Longinus (A.D. 213?–273), was also the first to draw an example of sublimity from the Hebrew scriptures.[10] In the nineteenth century Coleridge pronounced "Sublimity . . . Hebrew by birth" (Roston, 125).

Despite the comprehensive nature of Ishmael's quest to represent the whale, that quest is marked by an encounter with limits and a refusal to cross over the line and represent that which is unrepresentable. This refusal is primarily what distinguishes the structure of Ishmael's quest from Ahab's and it entails a deconstruction of two representational modes that depend on the position of an ultimate signifier: typology, inherited from medieval Christian interpretations of the Hebrew scriptures, and one-point perspective, rooted in Renaissance science and valorization of the self. The dismantling of these structures was already begun in conjunction with the rise of sublime aesthetics in the eighteenth and early nineteenth centuries.

4

THE LIMITS OF
TYPOLOGY

THE TELEOLOGY OF THE TYPOLOGICAL system developed by the Christians as a method of interpreting and appropriating the Hebrew scriptures points to an ultimate signifying God. The teleology of the system of linear perspective, which had dominated Western landscape painting since the Renaissance, points to an autonomous self reflected in the point on the horizon at which parallel lines converge on the two-dimensional surface of the canvas. Both typology and one-point perspective are linear, centralized, hierarchical structures. In the history of sublime aesthetics, we find precedence for Ishmael's problematization of both these teleological structures in his artistic quest for the sublime. Robert Lowth, a theorist and popularizer of sublime aesthetics in the eighteenth century, challenged the hegemony of biblical typological interpretation. In the nineteenth century American painters attempting to represent the sublimity of Niagara Falls broke with the age-old tradition of linear perspective. Melville's sublime needs to be situated against the backdrop of these critical developments and artistic innovations associated with the increasing interest in sublime aesthetics.

In his quest to represent the sublimity of the whale, Melville had to deal with many of the same formal problems of scale, detail, and point of view that faced the artist who attempted to paint the sublimity of the American landscape. Elizabeth McKinsey tells of how nineteenth-century American painters searching for a mode to represent the "rudeness" of the American landscape abandoned one-point perspective along with the dominant "picturesque" techniques of ordering nature (techniques associated with Claude Lorrain and popularized by William Gilpin involving the use of framing devices and the creation of three distinct picture planes). Many American artists, for example, in trying to capture the vast expanse and power of the nineteenth-century icon of the sublime, Niagara Falls, found these picturesque conventions imported from Europe to be woefully inadequate.

John Vanderlyn was one of the first painters to break with one-point perspective when he tried to recreate the effects of the panorama in his paintings of Niagara Falls. The panorama was a popular form of entertainment consisting of a long roll of canvas painted with some topographical scene of interest. To view a panorama, the audience would enter a room and be surrounded on all sides with the continuously changing stretch of canvas. Vanderlyn's experience with painting panoramas may have inspired him to eventually reject linear perspective in trying to capture the Falls. Discarding the traditional "45-degree rule," which required that the prospect of the painted scene be limited to one person's stationary view, Vanderlyn and other American artists after him who were caught up in the national fervor to represent the sublime, began to experiment with multiple points of view. The incorporation of multiple points of view in breaking with single-point perspective served to flatten the picture plane, pushing everything to the fore while calling attention to the two-dimensional surface of the canvas. This formal shift helped create not only the first paintings to convey the sublimity of the falls, but the first American art movement to capture the attention of the world's artistic community.[1]

The break with the structure of one-point perspective reflects a challenge to the autonomy of the self. In Melville's works this challenge to the self is intimately linked to a multiculturalism in which phallocentric and ethnocentric hegemony dissolves in a multivoiced dialogue. In *Moby-Dick* Melville employs several methods in breaking with one-point perspective to create a decentered, all-inclusive view that is analogous to the panoramic vistas of the American landscape painters. He repeatedly breaks the linear flow of the first-person narrative to open the text to different voices. At key moments, dramatic monologues and dialogues erase the presence of the narrator entirely. He also evokes the different voices and values of various genres, treating genres, such as the temperance tale, with an objectivity that is rooted in his cultural relativism.[2] At times, Melville breaks with his own words all together when he incorporates the texts of others in the spirit of collage. His use of the structure of the dual quests in *Moby-Dick* prefigures his later experiments with the diptych form in which he explores the relationship between two separate and contrasting scenes or points of view.

Throughout *Moby-Dick* structures of duplicity and multiplicity provide an alternative to the linearity of teleological structures. Ishmael's quest to represent the whale, for example, though linear in form, is marked by limits at which the teleological structure falls back on itself, a moment often marked on a rhetorical level by the figure of the oxymoron. The unsettling oscillation of the oxymoron represents Ishmael's antiteleological refusal to cross over into a transcendent realm beyond representation. This refusal has implications for interpretive practice. Ishmael's oxymoronic strategies represent a method of reading opposed to the linearity of typological interpretation.

One-point perspective in the visual arts is a method of reading nature, a method rooted in the humanistic and scientific approach to nature so characteristic of the Renaissance. One-point perspective imposes an order on nature. Typology, as a method for reading texts rooted in the Christian appropriation and subordination of the Hebrew scriptures, also represents an imposition. At the same time American painters were breaking with one-point perspective in their quest for the sublime, American writers were beginning to break with the practice of typology, which, for many of them, came to signify a form of "literary fascism" (Keller, 296). Nineteenth-century America, in contrast to Europe, was the scene of great typological innovation. The practice of typology in America is rooted in Calvinism. Of all the Protestant sects, Calvinists were most attracted to the Hebrew scriptures, and the practice of typology served to justify their preference (Brumm, 31). These Protestants went beyond the classical use of typology as a means to appropriate the Hebrew scriptures for Christianity. They deemphasized the historical quality of the antitype in keeping with their emphasis on the individual's relation to God. They rejected the Catholic doctrine of God's covenant with the church and replaced it with the idea of individual covenants. According to Ursula Brumm, the early American Puritans exploited the open-endedness of the typological structure that pointed to a future fulfillment beyond the antitype of the historical Christ, and they cast themselves in the position of the antitype (27). Typology became a means of interpreting and sanctifying individual everyday experience through the use of biblical types.

Perry Miller and Sacvan Bercovitch argue that typological interpretation in America was popular because it reassured the early Puritan settlers who had originally conceived of their settlement as an outpost of the Reformation. When the fall of Cromwell left them stranded, they restored their sense of mission through recourse to the practice of typological interpretation. They cast themselves as the people of Israel, in exodus from Egypt, sent by God into the wilderness to found a New Canaan (Miller, *Errand in the Wilderness*; Bercovitch, 5). The Puritan rhetoricians often took the renewal of this covenant with God as their theme, particularly on election day. In his study of the American Jeremiad, Bercovitch suggests that the teleological structure of typological interpretation must have been especially attractive to the new American colony because the colonists replaced the relatively static hierarchy of classes associated with the older European social structure with a teleological view of classes as stages (23). Brumm concludes that the favorite Puritan practice of linking individuals with biblical types is at the root of American democratic thought (178).

The appeal of typology's progressive, teleological structure seems to have carried over into a distinctly American view of the landscape, which Bercovitch traces in the shifting meanings of the word *frontier*. In Europe frontier traditionally referred to a border or limit dividing one people from another. For many Americans, frontier came to mean "a *figural* outpost, the outskirts of the advancing kingdom of God" and eventually served as a divine "summons to territorial expansion" in what was later referred to as America's "manifest destiny" (Bercovitch, 163–64). As the self progressively replaced Christ as the antitype in American typologies, nature began to replace scripture as the source of prophecy, especially for nineteenth-century New England transcendentalists. We also find countertraditions of typological interpretation, for example, among the Christian slaves who saw America as the Egypt out of which they prayed to be released, as the people of Israel did before them (Noll, 49).

According to Keller in his study of the use of typology in the American Renaissance, Melville is one of the authors disaffected with the practice of typology.[3] To better understand the role typology plays in *Moby-Dick* and in Ishmael's quest for the sublime, it is useful to consider the historical configuration that links the growing suspicion concerning the practice of typology with the growing interest in the aesthetics of the sublime. A key figure in this regard is Bishop Robert Lowth, the influential popularizer of Longinus's theory of the sublime who is generally credited with the "rediscovery" of biblical parallelism, the structural principle underlying Hebrew verse. In a series of lectures on the sacred poetry of the Hebrews given at Oxford from 1741 to 1751, Lowth advanced a new biblical translation technique by directing attention to the phenomenon of parallelism in Hebrew poetry. Lowth helped bring to an end the neoclassical method of translating the Bible according to an idea of poetry that depended on accentual or qualitative meter.

The rhythm of Hebrew verse is one of sense, not meter. Biblical parallelism subordinates form to content. Murray Roston, tracing the influence of Lowth's discovery on the development of Romantic poetic form, characterizes the effect of such parallelism as a "rhythmic ebb and flow, a sense which doubles back upon itself, rather than the linear forward movement of classical verse" (22). Lowth, in a lecture titled "The Sublime of Passion," identifies sublimity with the Hebrew tradition and argues for the Bible's superiority over the verse of his eighteenth-century neoclassical contemporaries (cited in Roston, 106). With the predominant emphasis in biblical studies on figural interpretation, or typology, scholars were slow to recognize the unique aesthetic qualities of biblical poetry. Roston argues that the typological method of reading the Bible, by limiting commentary to a search for figures beneath the literal surface of the Old Testament, blinded readers to the text's aesthetic qualities (42).[4] This blindness may also be the result of a structural discrepancy between the linear, teleological structure of typology and the nonformal parallelism that underlies biblical poetry. Lowth's interest in the aesthetics of the sublime and his recognition of biblical parallelism may indicate his receptivity in general to nonteleological structures.

In *Moby-Dick* we can trace an antagonism between the figural, or typological, method of interpretation and a method of interpretation based on an aesthetics of the sublime, an antagonism figured in the contrast between the quests of Ishmael and Ahab. In the opening line of the book, the narrator's invitation to the reader, "Call me Ishmael," situates the text in a peculiar relation to the long-standing tradition of typological interpretation in America, a tradition in which Americans used Old Testament biblical types to interpret themselves as God's chosen people enduring the harshness of the wilderness before passing into the promised land. What does it mean, in this context, for Melville's narrator to take the name of the one excluded from God's covenant with Abraham and his descendants in a country founded on the principles of Calvinist covenant theology? If covenant theology is basically a typological construct, in what way does Ishmael's exclusion from the covenant figure the status of typology in Melville's text?

Ursula Brumm and Karl Keller represent two opposing points of view concerning the significance of typology in *Moby-Dick* and the relation of Melville's work to the tradition of typological interpretation in America. In *American Thought and Religious Typology* Brumm begins by carefully distinguishing her project from Feidelson's *Symbolism in American Literature* because she feels Feidelson is guilty of situating Melville ahistorically within the context of the symbolists. Brumm argues for a placement of Melville within the historical tradition of the early Puritan typologists who believed that only God creates symbols. She claims that Melville "never doubted that the world with all its features was a divine creation. . . . For Melville, writing did not mean to create a world but to interpret the world." Brumm considers Melville a "symbolist realist" for whom the "actual world and experience are keys for a deeper, supernatural meaning." Although she admits he was "skeptical" (a statement hard to reconcile with her claim that he "never doubted"), Melville ultimately believed that "god uses real phenomena and events as signs for human beings." "If things had no significance," she argues, "Melville's writing would lose its point" (11, 196, 193).

Keller contends that Brumm's conclusions are the result of a faulty method. This method, which Brumm identifies as an extension of Auerbach's, consists of tracing the word "type" in its various uses since medieval times. This works fine, says Keller, in the seventeenth and eighteenth centuries when typology functioned as a system of ideas for the Puritans; it begins to lose its power, however, in the nineteenth century when typology loses its theological significance, but is retained as an artistic structure. The "original meaning" of the typological terms is replaced in the nineteenth century by "tension between the new meanings and the residue of (or allusion to) the old. We sense, then, the value of religious frames of reference for secular/aesthetic terms in nineteenth-century America. The secular retains a moral/spiritual tone." For Melville, Keller writes, the antitype is not a sense-giving divine presence as Brumm suggests, but is "always inscrutable." The world, for Melville, is "unavailable for types relating to it" (Brumm, 27; Keller, 281–82, 284, 297).

Melville's aesthetics of the sublime necessitates a refusal to cross over into the transcendent realm of the antitype and a resistance to carry through on the totalizing thrust of typology. When Keller concludes that authors like Melville came to see typology as a form of "literary fascism," he touches on the political implications of Melville's dismantling of typological structures (296). Although it may be true, as Brumm states, that the Puritan typological practice of linking individuals to biblical types represents a move toward greater democratization, the individualist ideology at the root of this practice, when linked to covenant theology, works to justify the oppression of those excluded from God's covenant, like the unconverted indigenous population of America.[5]

This is the context we need to keep in mind when reading the opening line of *Moby-Dick*, "Call me Ishmael." In a country where many see themselves in terms of the typology of covenant theology, as God's chosen people, Ishmael's act is both a call for the reader to interpret the text typologically and a statement of the impossibility of such an interpretation. The name Melville chooses is rich with typological determinations, yet those determinations already signify an absence of determination, an absence of ties figured in the biblical Ishmael's exclusion from God's covenant and his father's inheritance. The name Ishmael points to a position both inside and outside the structure of typological interpretation. Because Melville's Ishmael names himself, he is both inside and outside language's determining power. Ishmael enters the book in the act of breaking all ties to the shore, to family, and to country. His exclusion from the covenant, however, is a kind of freedom: it frees him to establish an alternative, and more inclusive, covenant in the form of a marriage contract with the pagan Polynesian harpooner, Queequeg. They seal their bond by equally distributing Queequeg's money between them, pledging mutual devotion, and worshiping Queequeg's black idol together. Melville's subversion of the typology of covenant theology allows for a vision of democracy beyond the radical individualism of the Puritans: a vision of a democracy of multiculturalism and egalitarianism.

Ahab, the other major character in *Moby-Dick* named after a figure in the Old Testament, at first glance seems to be an example of the rhetorical figure antonomania, in which a proper name is used to stand for a type. If this were a case of antonomania, however, the captain of the *Pequod* would be referred to as "an Ahab," a figure meant to recall (as Ishmael recalls when he hears the name) the wicked king whose blood was licked by dogs. But Ahab is not *an* Ahab, Ahab *is* Ahab. And perhaps most importantly, Ahab did not, like Ishmael, name himself. According to the story told by Peleg: "Twas a foolish, ignorant whim of his crazy, widowed mother, who died when he was only a twelve-month old, And yet the old squaw Tistig, at Gay-head, said that the name would somehow prove prophetic" (77).

Ahab's name signifies a kind of determination, the determination of language, from which there is no escape. In Brumm's typological interpretation of Ahab's name, she apparently forgets for a moment Peleg's story and wonders whether the name is a surname or a given name. She then goes on to declare that "in fact no Puritan or Quaker ever named a son after an infamous biblical personage annihilated by God. This would be tantamount to a prophecy of damnation for the hapless child" (179). But such a thing is certainly possible, and in the world of Melville's book, at least, happened.

Both Ahab and Ishmael are types of exclusion and as such represent the negative aspect of typological interpretation. In spite of Eric Auerbach's valiant efforts in his essay "Figura" to prove that typology does not destroy the type in favor of the antitype, but preserves it in its full historical determination, Christian history tells a different story. We have already seen how the tendency to read the Hebrew scripture as merely a repository of types to be fulfilled in the New Testament resulted in blinding readers to the text's individual aesthetic qualities. The Hebrew scriptures are often seen as the "old" Testament, to be superseded by the "new" (and presumably improved). The teleological structure of figural interpretation necessarily entails exclusion and subordination. Such structures need to be dismantled to create a truly multicultural and egalitarian democratic perspective. Significantly, the one who predicts that Ahab's name will prove to be his fate is a Native American. As a woman and an Amerindian, Tistig is a doubly determined figure of exclusion in American society.

In terms of Christian typology, Ahab's exclusion is absolute; he is aligned with the exclusion in the Bible of the forces of evil. Ishmael's status as a result of his exclusion from God's covenant with Abraham is more problematic; he was after all "blessed." In *Moby-Dick,* because Ishmael names himself, his exclusion amounts to a kind of freedom. And although his name signifies an absence of ties, Ishmael is free to form a loving tie with Queequeg. Ahab, on the other hand, is anything but free, and he ends up breaking all ties but one: the line he fastens to Moby Dick, which wraps around his neck. "The path to my fixed purpose is laid with iron rails, whereon my soul is grooved to run," says Ahab. "Naught's an obstacle, naught's an angle to the iron way!" (168). Teleologically determined to one end, Ahab is a figure for the structure of typology. The relationship between figure and fulfillment in typological interpretation is analogous to the deterministic relationship between cause and effect, which constitutes one of the polar propositions in Kant's antinomy of pure reason.

Once the teleological structure of typology is set in motion, a final and original cause must be assumed in order to avoid falling into the abyss of infinite progress/regress. If empty skepticism is rejected, the search for a final/first cause leads inevitably to an end that governs the relationship between the events in time. In the history of typology we find that end located outside of time and space in an all-determining Being who creates and redeems meaning. But how does something determine the relationships between figure and fulfillment if it is completely outside that determining sphere? We can see Ahab struggling with these philosophical questions the day before he catches up with Moby Dick, when he asks:

> What is it, what nameless, inscrutable, unearthly thing is it, what cozening, hidden lord and master, and cruel, remorseless emperor commands me; that against all natural lovings and longings, I so keep pushing, and crowding, and jamming myself on all the time recklessly making me ready to do what in my own proper, natural heart, I durst not so much as dare? Is Ahab, Ahab? Is it I, God, or who, that lifts this arm? But if the great sun move not of himself,

but is an errand-boy in heaven; nor one single star can revolve, but by some invisible power; how then can this one small heart beat; this one small brain think thoughts; unless God does that beating, does that thinking, does that living, and not I. By heaven, man, we are turned round and round in this world, like yonder windlass, and Fate is the handspike. And all the time, lo! that smiling sky, and this unsounded sea! Look! see yon Albicore! who put it into him to chase and fang that flying-fish? Where do murderers go, man! Who's to doom, when the judge himself is dragged to the bar? (545)

Ahab is a figure for typology in a world where there is no final redemption. Ahab's dilemma becomes even more complex as it takes on a moral dimension. Ahab is a biblical type of evil. His act of personifying evil in the whale becomes a projection, an attempt to exorcise evil in himself. Is Ahab, Ahab, he asks. In being named for the evil king of old, is Ahab himself a personification of evil? Wrong not Ahab because he has a wicked name. Ahab, unlike Ishmael, "did not name himself" (79). But has Ahab's name determined Ahab's fate as Tistig predicted it would?

Ahab's story is a tragedy. His use of metaphors borrowed from theater and war when he speaks to Starbuck on the second day of the chase for Moby Dick suggests that he sees his role as determined by forces outside him: "This whole act's immutably decreed. 'Twas rehearsed by thee and me a billion years before this ocean rolled. Fool! I am the Fates' lieutenant; I act under orders." The vision that Ahab is able to articulate so brilliantly and beautifully is in the end a severely limited one as Ahab progressively grows blind (561, 528). In the typological world Ahab inhabits, a world in which the name has such determining power, where lies the possibility of human freedom?

This is the dilemma Kant tries to solve by positing a distinction between appearances and things-in-themselves, a distinction that Ahab seems unwilling or unable to grant when he exclaims, "How immaterial are all materials! What things real are there, but imponderable thoughts" (528). In his "pasteboard mask" speech, Ahab seems to think that by driving his harpoon into Moby Dick he can pierce through the phenomenal realm into the noumenal:

Hark ye yet again,—the little lower layer. All visible objects, man, are but as pasteboard masks. But in each event—in the living act, the undoubted deed—there, some unknown but still reasoning

thing puts forth the mouldings of its features from behind the un-
reasoning mask. If man will strike, strike through the mask! How
can the prisoner reach outside except by thrusting through the
wall? To me, the white whale is that wall, shoved near to me. Sometimes I think there's naught beyond. But 'tis enough. He tasks me;
He heaps me; I see in him outrageous strength, with an inscrutable malice sinewing it. That inscrutable thing is chiefly what I
hate; and be the white whale agent, or be the white whale princi-
pal, I will wreak that hate upon him. (164)

Ahab, like Ishmael before the face that is no face, experiences the white
whale as a limit to his powers of understanding—like a wall shoved up
against him. But unlike Ishmael, Ahab feels imprisoned.

The more Ahab tries to free himself by "thrusting through the wall,"
the more enslaved he becomes. Ahab is imprisoned by the structure of
representation itself. Ishmael, no less appalled than Ahab by the white
whale, manages a different kind of escape from his dilemma by negating
the logic of representation through recourse to the oxymoronic rhetoric of the sublime. At the margins of typology, Ishmael circumvents the
totalizing thrust of teleological structures. Through his use of the oxymoron and multiple points of view, he directs attention to the limits of
representation and challenges the reduction of multiplicity and difference that characterizes teleological thought in general.

5

FANATICISM

IN CREATING AN ART that embodies the values of an egalitarian and heterogeneous democratic society, Melville represents traditional artistic structures like typology and one-point perspective as aesthetic analogues to the politics of totalitarianism. To the politics of democracy, on the other hand, Melville posits an aesthetic closely related to the Kantian sublime. Melville's sublime destabilizes the ultimate signifier/telos (God or the self) and dismantles or recasts totalizing structures from a marginal, decentered perspective. Lyotard has found the same antitotalitarian thrust in his readings of Kant's "heterogeneous sublime."[1] The totalitarian energy in *Moby-Dick* centers around Ahab, and his monomania contrasts sharply with Ishmael's openness and relativism. The difference between the two positions of Ahab and Ishmael is crucial to an understanding of the relation between politics and aesthetics in the book. Although many have treated this contrast before, there is still something to be gained by situating their respective positions within the context of sublime aesthetics.[2] With the help of Kant's theory of the sublime, we can explore the metaphysics of Ahab's monomania and see how Melville's critique of aesthetic ideology in *Moby-Dick* reflects his democratic values.

According to Kant, the monomaniac, or fanatic, collapses the distinction between phenomena and noumena. Kant defines fanaticism as a "belief in our capacity of seeing something beyond all bounds of sensibility." Fanatics like Ahab do not acknowledge the limits to their powers of representation. Because they think they can see what is beyond all bounds of sensibility, they come to believe in the positive presentation of moral ideas, just as Ahab believes that Moby Dick is the personification of all evil. Kant calls this "going mad with reason." Ahab crosses the line that Ishmael refuses to cross, that is, the line that marks the realm of the transcendent and that separates, in Kantian terms, empirical phenomena from the ideas of reason. The noumenon must be beyond representation in any positive sense. In Melville and Kant this proposition takes on the quality of a moral imperative. There are, according to Kant, political repercussions to the act of positively presenting moral ideas like God and evil (*Judgment*, 116).

Kant resolved the antinomy between the concept of causality and the concept of freedom by positing the distinction between appearances, or phenomena, which can be known but only as conditioned by our sense of time and space, and things-in-themselves, or noumena, which can be thought but not known and can only be negatively represented. With this distinction Kant breaks the dogmatic hold of empiricism.[3] This distinction between phenomena and noumena must be maintained, according to Kant, in order to preserve the possibility of freedom from the determinations of causality. The concept of freedom is finally, for Kant, the *only* thing that can be known of the noumena or supersensuous world. The subject in Kant cannot be reduced to one; it is both noumenon, a free, self-determining "thing-in-itself," and a determined phenomenon (*Practical Reason*, 73; see also chapter 2).

The totalitarian threat to freedom that arises when the distinction between phenomena and noumena is collapsed and ideas like God and evil are presented as empirical phenomena, is illustrated in *Moby-Dick* by the conditions aboard the *Pequod* and the *Jeroboam*. Ahab creates a fascistlike state when he personifies all evil in the white whale and so does Gabriel, the "Shaker prophet of the *Jeroboam*" who sees the white whale as the "Shaker God incarnated" (316). The two mirror each other. It makes little difference whether the white whale is seen as evil or as God—both interpretations abolish freedom in their fanaticism.

In contrast to fanaticism, the sublime's mode of presentation in Kant's theory is "quite negative in respect of what is sensible." Because the sublime marks the limits to our powers of representation, it is "incompatible" with fanaticism's transgression of those limits. By its "very abstraction," Kant writes, the sublime is a "presentation of the Infinite, which can be nothing but a mere negative presentation." It is by means of this negativity that the sublime "expands the soul." In captaining the ship Ahab is like the politicians Kant chastises for encouraging positive presentations of morality. Such governments, Kant writes, keep their people "mere passive beings by arbitrarily assigning limits to the extension of their spiritual powers." As long as ideas are merely presented negatively, there is no danger of fanaticism. It is in this aesthetic-political context that Kant praises the sublimity of the Hebrew law banning representation (*Judgment*, 115, 116).

We have already noted the similarities between Kant's negation and the negative moment in Melville's aesthetic when he writes to Hawthorne, "take God out of the dictionary, and you would have Him in the street." This is the moment of saying "NO! in thunder" that Melville outlines in the same letter. Melville's praise of Hawthorne is traditionally read as a rejection of sentimentalism and conventional morality. Indeed, the freedom to write unfettered by moral constraints was crucial for Melville. This artistic freedom enabled him to write his "wicked book" and still feel "spotless as the lamb." But saying "NO! in thunder" needs to be considered in the broader representational context provided by the aesthetics of the sublime as a declaration of the limits to representation and a refusal to represent the unrepresentable in any way but negatively. In the letter from which "NO! in thunder" is extracted, we find Melville pondering the "tragicalness of human thought," a phrase expressive of the tragic tension between the finitude of human existence and the infinitude of human thought. When Melville, talking of our relationship to "God," pulls back and reflects on his use of that word and declares this "*Being* of the matter . . . the knot with which we choke ourselves," his words point to the knot in *Moby-Dick* with which the fanatic Ahab literally chokes himself as the result of his quest to destroy "all evil" as personified in the white whale. By representing an unrepresentable totality, by collapsing the distinction between unrepresentable ideas and empirical phenomenon, Ahab relinquishes the possibility of freedom (*Letters*, 125, 142, 124).

Saying "NO! in thunder" is not so much Melville aligning himself with the forces of "evil." After all, Melville writes in his letter, "the Devil himself cannot make him say *yes*." As a declaration of the limits to representation, "NO! in thunder" is also a declaration of equality with and independence from all the "powers of heaven, hell, and earth." The result is freedom as described in the following passage: "All men who say *yes,* lie; and all men who say *no,* —why, they are in the happy condition of judicious, unincumbered travellers in Europe; they cross the frontiers into Eternity with nothing but a carpet-bag, — that is to say, the Ego. Whereas those *yes*-gentry, they travel with heaps of baggage, and damn them! they will never get through the Custom House. What's the reason, Mr. Hawthorne, that in the last stages of metaphysics a fellow always falls to *swearing* so?" Perhaps because "swearing," in this case, indicates that moment of negation before the transcendent, the last stages of metaphysics when we come face to face with our limits. Beyond those limits lies the stuff of metaphysics, the ideas that can only be represented negatively by marking those limits (*Letters,* 124–25).

When Ahab represents the white whale as all evil visibly personified, his quest takes on the teleological structure of a moral crusade. His subordination of the whale to the purposes of morality resembles the subordination of nature to God's purpose represented in the whalemen's chapel painting of the moral sublime. In his fanaticism Ahab merely carries this moral sublime to its logically egoistic and solipsistic extreme. The closure that characterizes this version of the sublime is to be distinguished from the antitotalitarian, antiteleological thrust of Ishmael's sublime. The sublime in Melville and Kant is characterized by a refusal to cross the line into the transcendent and subordinate the nonrepresentable sublime to utilitarian purposes, or an all-powerful governing self or God. The moral sublime is a response to the threat many Americans saw as the atheistic, immoral implications of a sublime like Melville's. In the following passage from one of Emerson's early lectures extolling the sublime in a poem by Herbert, we can see why Melville might want to distance himself from Emerson's particular brand of transcendentalism. For Emerson, Herbert's poem represents "poetry . . . turned over to its noblest use" (*Early Lectures,* 352–53):

> The sea which seems to stop the travellor
> Is by a ship a speedier passage made.
> The winds who think they rule the mariner
> Are ruled by him and taught to serve his trade.

The poem represents a secular-humanistic version of the moral sublime comparable to the Christian version in the chapel painting. In praising the subordination of the ocean to the purposes of man, and also the subordination of poetry to the purposes of morality, Emerson is making what Kant would call a teleological judgment, not an aesthetic judgment of the sublime.

The sublime judgment is both antiteleological and anti-utilitarian. No knowledge can be generated from it because it marks a limit to the powers of understanding and to epistemology itself. When Kant illustrates the difference between the sublime and the teleological judgments, he shows how the same object, the ocean in this case, can be represented according to these two different perspectives:

> If we are to call the sight of the ocean sublime, we must not *think* of it as we [ordinarily] do, as implying all kinds of knowledge (that are not contained in immediate intuition). For example, we sometimes think of the ocean as a vast kingdom of aquatic creatures, or as the source of those vapors that fill the air with clouds for the benefit of the land, or again as an element which, though dividing continents from each other, yet promotes the greatest communication between them; but these furnish merely teleological judgments. To call the ocean sublime we must regard it as poets do, merely by what strikes the eye—if it is at rest, as a clear mirror of water only bounded by the heaven; if it is restless, as an abyss threatening to overwhelm everything. (*Judgment,* 110–11)

The subject and predicate of the teleological judgment are bound in Kant's example in a way unlike the formal link furnished by the analogy in the judgment of the sublime. The subordination that occurs in the teleological judgment by means of the concept of purpose makes possible knowledge and the exploitation of nature for man's needs. On the other hand, the aesthetical judgment "contributes nothing towards the knowledge of its objects." Aesthetic judgments, like the judgment of the sublime, are characterized by "formal purposiveness"; they contain no determined concept at their base. In characterizing the aesthetic judgment as "purposive without purpose," Kant himself must resort to the oxymoron, Ishmael's favorite rhetorical figure, to mark these limits (*Judgment,* 31).

In his quest to represent the whale, Ishmael engages many different methods of interpretation. Even when he conducts an "objective" scientific study, as in the cetology section, however, he is careful to mark the limits to his powers of representing the whale. He subverts the teleological thrust of his inquiry by acknowledging the incompleteness of all such systems. Although Melville's sublime needs to be distinguished from the teleology of the moral sublime, the distinction must be drawn carefully. The antiteleological and anti-utilitarian thrust of Melville's sublime does not necessarily preclude a political-ethical dimension to his aesthetic.

With the distinction between teleological and aesthetic judgments, we can analyze the way in which Ishmael's interpretive perspective differs from those of the other characters. *Moby-Dick* contains an array of interpretive methods to be assessed for their political-ethical implications. The perspective of utilitarianism, for example, is represented by Starbuck and the minor character Bildad. For Starbuck, the white whale is never the object of a specific quest as it is for Ishmael or Ahab. Starbuck sees Moby Dick as just another whale to be hunted for profit. Both Bildad and Starbuck contain in their names reference to their ultimate allegiance and the utilitarian's telos: the almighty dollar is "dad" and guiding light, or "star," all rolled into one. Starbuck is "game" for the white whale, he tells Ahab, "if it fairly comes in the way of the business we follow. . . . How many barrels will thy vengeance yield thee?" Ahab rightly sees that for the utilitarian Starbuck "money's to be the measurer." Starbuck's utilitarianism renders him morally impotent. The first mate may talk morality in the name of religion when he accuses Ahab of blasphemy for seeking revenge on a "dumb brute," but his morality is but a thinly disguised work ethic, and his ideal is money. Starbuck may be Ahab's only foil on board the ship, but critics who see in him a heroic representative of democratic thought are perhaps being lulled by the sound of a familiar voice in American culture that has come to seem the "voice of right reason," that is, the voice of corporate interests. Starbuck is a figure for liberalism, but he is not to be identified with the democratic heart of the text.[4] In the end, as Ishmael writes, the motley crew, made up of "mongrel renegades, and castaways, and cannibals," could only be "morally enfeebled . . . by the incompetence of mere unaided virtue or right-mindedness in Starbuck." Starbuck's liberal utilitarianism is ineffectual against Ahab's terrible fanaticism (163, 186).

The only interpretive perspective that truly challenges Ahab's fanaticism is Ishmael's. Ishmael's perspective does not fully develop until after the destruction of the *Pequod* at the end of the book. While on board the ship, Ishmael was one with the crew, Ahab's feud seemed his. In writing his book, however, Ishmael distances himself from Ahab's fanaticism and his own passive complicity. Ishmael, the author—not Starbuck—represents the book's democratic heart. The shift in Ishmael's interpretive perspective occurs after he experiences the sublime power of nature in the *Pequod*'s destruction. Evidence of this shift can be found in the ironic tone of Ishmael's account of his earlier "impatience" with Queequeg's "ridiculous Ramadan." Whereas the younger Ishmael seems to believe his lecture about the "progress of primitive religions" is for Queequeg's own good, the narrator's ironic tone suggests some distance from Ishmael's disrespect for his friend's boundaries (85). Melville's heterogeneous sublime represents an alternative to Ahab's totalitarian cult of personality. *Moby-Dick*'s primary conflict, in terms of aesthetic-political philosophy, is between Ishmael's sublime and Ahab's fanaticism.

After Ishmael explores what the white whale means to Ahab, he reflects on his own motives for joining in the chase. It was the color of the whale, its whiteness "that above all things appalled" Ishmael. In "The Whiteness of the Whale" Ishmael attempts to explain what this color means to him "else all these chapters might be naught" (188):

> Is it that by its indefiniteness it shadows forth the heartless voids and immensities of the universe, and thus stabs us from behind with the thought of annihilation when beholding the white depths of the milky way? Or is it, that as in essence whiteness is not so much a color as the visible absence of color, and at the same time the concrete of all colors; is it for these reasons that there is such a dumb blankness, full of meaning, in a wide landscape of snows—a colorless all-color of atheism from which we shrink? (195)

Ishmael must rely on the figure of the oxymoron to capture whiteness as the "dumb blankness full of meaning" and "the colorless all-color of atheism." His oxymoronic discourse marking the limits to his powers of representation stands in direct contrast to Ahab's personification of evil. In his zeal to represent the whale, Ishmael approaches the moment of personification, but, in contrast to Ahab, he doubles back at the sight of the face that is "no face." Ishmael's Moby Dick is sublime, that is, unable to be appropriated in any sense but negatively.

Kant defines the sublime as "an object (of nature) the representation of which determines the mind to think the unattainability of nature regarded as a presentation of ideas." The sublime is "that, the mere ability to think which, shows a faculty of mind surpassing every standard of sense." Nature is considered sublime, writes Kant, "in those of its phenomena whose intuition brings with it the idea of its infinity." The state of mind Kant calls sublime is triggered by the "formlessness" of nature. This formlessness is not so much a quality of the object (Kant is careful to avoid the empirical trap of locating the sublime in any object) as it is an indicator of the moment in the sublime judgment when the faculty of imagination fails to represent the object in its totality. To imagination (the faculty responsible for processing sensory data), the excessively large or powerful seems formless because it cannot be grasped and contained. When imagination is faced with such limitlessness beyond its powers of representation, reason steps in with its idea of totality to check imagination's ceaseless striving (*Judgment,* 108, 89, 94).

Reason's primary function is that of thinking the idea of "totality," an idea that cannot be derived empirically. For example, the faculty of reason in Kant's philosophy can think infinity as a totality. The sublime is characterized by conflict between imagination and reason, in contrast to the beautiful, which represents harmony between the imagination and understanding (both empirical faculties). This conflict between the empirical faculty of imagination and the rational faculty of reason, Kant calls a "vibration," an oscillation between two poles of attraction and repulsion. On the one hand, the mind is repulsed: for imagination, the faculty responsible for measuring sensory data, "the transcendent" toward which it is impelled is "like an abyss in which it fears to lose itself." On the other hand, the mind is also attracted: for the faculty of reason, the faculty responsible for thinking totality, the "idea of the supersensible" is not transcendent and imagination's effort appears "in conformity with law" (*Judgment,* 97).

For Kant, the experience of the sublime is "cognate" to "moral feeling," because the subject feels "hindrances" on the level of sensibility and imagination at the same time that it feels "superiority" to those hindrances by their subjugation. Even if the object appears in "opposition to our own (sensible) interests," it is making us aware of a faculty of our mind, reason, that is free from the determining influences of natural causality. The sublime prepares the groundwork for moral feeling by demonstrating, on an aesthetic level, the difference between the phenomenal and noumenal realms and thereby preserving the possibility of self-determination. It also prepares us to respect something, the object triggering the sublime in this case, even if it lies in opposition to our own immediate sensible interests (*Judgment*, 107, 108).

Not everyone will judge the same object sublime. Fanatics, for example, cannot appreciate the sublime because they collapse the distinction between phenomena and noumena. The power of Kant's theory of the sublime lies in the radical discontinuity between these two realms. Kant's theory cannot simply be "purged of its idealist metaphysics"— as semiotician Thomas Weiskel attempts in his skeptical search for a " 'realist' or psychological account" of the sublime—without considerable loss of power (23). The "inscrutableness of the idea of freedom," writes Kant, "cuts it off from any positive presentation" (*Judgment*, 116). When Weiskel calls sublime aesthetics necessarily "apolitical" (46), he neglects to consider that by demonstrating the possibility of our self-determination through reason and our freedom from the laws of causality, the sublime demonstrates the possibility of political action itself and, as Lyotard argues, the opposition to totalitarianism.

Of all the characters in *Moby-Dick*, only Ishmael judges the white whale sublime. If the white whale represents the unrepresentable in nature, then he should, according to Kant, trigger the sublime state of mind indicating a supersensible realm of ideas that can only be negatively represented. That Moby Dick *should* trigger the experience of the sublime does not mean that he necessarily *will* in everyone. According to Kant, in order to appreciate the sublime one must be predisposed to moral feeling, that is, the feeling that enables us to respect something even if it is in opposition to our own sensible interests (*Judgment*, 107–9).

The juxtaposition of Ishmael's view of the white whale with Ahab's corresponds in the book to the juxtaposition of Pip's view of the doubloon with Ahab's. Pip, in terms of his oxymoronic discourse, functions as Ishmael's surrogate in Ahab's drama. Ahab's only hope of salvation in the book lies not in the first mate Starbuck, who as a utilitarian participates in the same teleological structure as Ahab, but in that "most insignificant member of the crew," the slave boy and castaway, Pip, who occupies a marginal position in relation to the rest of the crew. In "The Castaway" Ishmael traces the development of Pip's particular interpretive perspective to his experience of being left by Stubb to float alone in the ocean for hours with no one in sight. Here we find Pip's turning point. In this sublime setting, alone in the ocean, Pip's "ringed horizon began to expand around him miserably. . . . By the merest chance," the ship rescued him, but the "infinite of his soul" had been "drowned" by the sea (414).

> Not drowned entirely, though. Rather carried down alive to wondrous depths, where strange shapes of the unwarped primal world glided to and fro before his passive eyes; and the miser-merman, Wisdom, revealed his hoarded heaps; and among the joyous, heartless, ever-juvenile eternities, Pip saw the multitudinous, God-omnipresent, coral insects, that out of the firmament of waters heaved the colossal orbs. He saw God's foot upon the treadle of the loom, and spoke it; and therefore his shipmates called him mad. So man's insanity is heaven's sense; and wandering from all mortal reason, man comes at last to that celestial thought, which, to reason, is absurd and frantic; and weal or woe, feels then uncompromised, indifferent as his God. (414)

Ishmael and Pip are linked by their experience of the sublime. Ishmael identifies himself with Pip in this chapter when he recounts Pip's experience alone on the ocean and says we shall see "what like abandonment befell myself" (414). Both Ishmael and Pip are castaways. Both have journeyed to the outer limits and returned. Ishmael defers to Pip by granting him the last word at two crucial moments in the text: at the end of the dramatic sequence before Ishmael reenters the text as first-person narrator and at the end of the chapter on the doubloon.

In "The Doubloon" Melville presents a compendium of judgments corresponding in type to the array of judgments of the white whale. In showing how the same object can be interpreted according to different perspectives, Melville is proposing his own "Copernican revolution" by directing our attention to the constructed nature of representation itself. Melville, like Kant, challenges empirical dogmatism by reflecting on the perceptual apparatus and the mechanism of interpretation. He extends Kant's notion of the split subject to include a variety of individual perspectives, thereby breaking with one-point perspective. The set of interpretations about the doubloon begins "in a monomaniac way" with the one who nailed the coin to the mast, aiming to fix the crew in his quest for Moby Dick.

Ahab's method of interpretation is typological personification, with himself in the role of antitype. The coin holds only one meaning for Ahab: Ahab is the volcano; Ahab is the undaunted fowl; Ahab is the firm tower. The coin, according to Ahab, is like the round globe that merely "mirrors back" man's (namely Ahab's) "own mysterious self." Next before the coin, Starbuck reads according to the Christian typological tradition, regarding nature as a type or shadow of the divine. He sees "some faint earthly symbol" of the trinity in the three mountain peaks. The sun, within Starbuck's typological scheme, stands for God's righteousness. Starbuck reveals his characteristic moral weakness when he finds the thought of the sunless night unbearable and turns away from the coin "lest Truth," he says, "shake me falsely." Stubb pulls out his almanac to interpret the signs of the zodiac as an allegory of man's life. Flask sees only the coin's exchange value for cigars. The old Manxman accurately predicts the *Pequod*'s disastrous fate by reading, in conjunction with the coin, the horseshoe nailed to the opposite side of the mast. The next two non-Western interpreters before the coin remain silent: Queequeg compares the marks on his body to the inscriptions on the coin and Fedallah bows down before it in worship (431, 432).

Finally, Pip focuses on the act of perception prior to the formation of meaning: "I look, you look, he looks; we look, ye look, they look." The subject of the sentence shifts as he moves through all grammatically possible points of view. After this multiperspectival introduction, Pip refers to the coin as the "ship's navel." For Pip, the coin represents "aught." "When aught's nailed to the mast," he says, "it's a sign that things grow desperate." Pip associates the coin with the notion of covenant. The coin nailed to the mast reminds him of the time when his father cut down a tree and found a "darkey's wedding ring" embedded in it. Pip predicts that instead of Ahab nailing the white whale as he nailed the coin, the white whale will "nail" him and the coin on the mast will sink to the bottom of the sea, only to be redeemed "in the resurrection" (434, 435).

The rhetoric of multiplicity in Ishmael's opening discussion of the doubloon's history—its origin in the "duplicitous" Ecuador midway up the Andes—mirrors Pip's reading of the coin at the end of the chapter. The image of the doubloon as "navel"—marking both an origin and an end and at the same time an absence, "aught"—corresponds structurally to Ishmael's oxymoronic formulation of the whiteness of the whale as the "colorless all-color of atheism." The navel recalls a primary division into two as it marks the biological tie linking the mother and the child. The ties that link us socially with one another in our autonomy and interdependence are suggested also by Pip's reference to the marriage covenant. This fundamental multiplicity, the monomaniacal Ahab must reduce to one.

Significantly, Ahab uses a coin, symbol of the homogenization of capital, to subsume his crew under the telos of his quest. Ahab's intolerance for the duplicitous oxymoron is apparent in his response to Queequeg's coffin-turned-life-buoy. "Here now's the very dreaded symbol of grim death, by a mere hap, made the expressive sign of the help and hope of most endangered life." He curses the sound of the carpenter's hammer hitting the lid. "What in all things makes the sounding-board is this," he says to the carpenter; "there's naught beneath." Ahab cannot abide the oxymoron's indeterminacy, the vibration between poles of meaning that negates the fixing of any one meaning. Ahab orders the carpenter to "let me not see that thing here when I return again" (528, 529).

Ahab's use of the doubloon as a telos to focus and fix his crew has the fascistic effect of making one out of many. The coin was "set apart and sanctified to one awe-striking end" by the crew who "revered it as the white whale's talisman." It points to the end of the chase when the appearance of Moby Dick will fulfill the promise of the coin's redemption. According to Ahab's calculated prediction, that redemption will occur on the Season-on-the-Line, a point located on the equator, on the opposite side of the globe from Ecuador where the doubloon was minted. On the face of the coin, the sun enters the zodiac at the "equinoctial point of Libra." These facts Ishmael gives concerning the "equatorial" nature of the coin stress the doubloon's "doubleness" as a locus of value. The "centrality" of the "equatorial coin" cannot be reduced to one; it always already implies a multiplicity—as the equator is not so much the center of the world as it is a line dividing the totality into two parts, or more properly speaking, three parts, if we count the line itself (431).

In the chapter titled "The Line," Ishmael tells the reader that attention to the line is necessary for a "better understanding" of the whale scenes. He precisely traces in a long paragraph the whale line's machinations on board the whale boat until its "sundry mystifications" become "too tedious to detail." I take this chapter as an invitation to trace the line or thematics of line in the book, at the risk of tedium. What we will find is that again the linear structure of teleology is subverted by the antiteleological thrust of Ishmael's aesthetics of the sublime. In chapter 3 I discussed how Ishmael's attempt to represent the whale and Ahab's quest to destroy it are linked through the imagery of the line when Ishmael compares the conceptualizing of whales, the linking of types with names, to the hopeless attempt to draw out the leviathan with a hook and line in order to make a covenant with him. In Ishmael's systematization of whales there will always be lines that cannot be fastened to whales, discrepancies between names and things, remainders that leave the system incomplete. Like the unfinished Cathedral of Cologne, "grand" systems, "true ones, . . . ever leave the copestone to posterity" (240, 145).

By following his chapter on the whiteness of the whale with the chapter titled "The Chart," Ishmael is again contrasting his methods and Ahab's. We learn that Ahab hopes to locate on his map that "particular set time and place . . . [where] all possibilities would become probabilities . . . [and] every possibility the next thing to a certainty." The fanatic Ahab is shown in his cabin poring over his maps, intently studying and tracing lines "over spaces that before were blank, . . . threading a maze of currents and eddies, with a view to the more certain accomplishment of that monomaniac thought of his soul" (200, 198–99).

Ishmael, however, writes in his biography of Queequeg that "true places" are never on maps. Ahab's science may succeed in leading him to the white whale, but Moby Dick is the one whale that cannot be fastened to without the threat of death or dismemberment. To fasten the line to the white whale is to self-destruct because it signifies crossing the boundary that marks our limits, the boundary that Kant enforces for the sake of our own freedom and the possibility of a community based on respect for difference. The book's imagery of the line appears also as a loving link between people. Ishmael is tied to Queequeg by the monkey-rope, and in the chapter "The Log and Line" Ahab tells Pip, "thou art tied to me by cords woven of my heart-strings." Ahab ultimately breaks those strings and all ties to humanity in his quest to fasten to Moby Dick. The dismemberment that results from Ahab's initial encounter with the white whale is not only a loss of limb, but a loss of membership in the community, an act with disastrous results for the members of his present community, the crew that he considers merely the means to his own ends, the "tools" he will use to accomplish his one object (53, 522, 211).[5]

Ahab's fate—to be strangled by the whale line he fastens to Moby Dick—is significantly sealed by an interpretive act: his interpretation of Fedallah's prophecy leads him to believe in his own immortality on land and sea. The prophecy states that before Ahab can die he must "verily" see "two hearses" on the sea: "the first" must not be "made by mortal hands; and the visible wood of the last must be grown in America." Ahab simply dismisses this first part of Fedallah's prophecy because he cannot imagine ever seeing "such a strange sight [as] a hearse and its plumes floating over the ocean with the waves for pall-bearers." Ahab also dismisses the second part of the prophecy, that "hemp only can kill thee," when he interprets hemp as referring to the gallows. The prophecy proves true and Ahab is doomed, in a sense, by his limited "literalist" reading of the word "hearse" and his inability to consider "hemp" in its various uses. The two hearses turn out to be Moby Dick carrying the dead body of Fedallah and the stoved ship carrying the crew to the bottom of the sea. The hemp refers to the whale line that Ahab attaches to Moby Dick, the line that wraps around Ahab's neck and strangles him (499).

Fedallah's prophecy brings together on the thematic level of interpretation several strands in our reading of *Moby-Dick* and the sublime. In its image of the hearse "not made by mortal hands," the prophecy requires Ahab to recognize a nature outside human means and ends. The second hearse made of wood grown in America recalls America's appropriation of the natural "sublime" for the technological purposes of man. And the "hemp" image brings us back to the thematics of the line. The line in the book can either signify a marriage based on mutual empowerment and respect for difference or, when it is used for making typological connections, a power over and subordination of the other, and an erasure of difference. Ahab's monomania restricts him to the latter use of the line. He determines objects as he himself is determined, fixed and fastened to one end, one meaning. Through his personification of evil in Moby Dick, Ahab hopes to bridge the abyss that in Kant's system is unbridgeable in any positive sense, the abyss separating ideas (the realm of freedom) from phenomena (the realm of natural causality).

When Ahab sucks all around him down into the abyss at the end of his quest, two objects escape the total, systematic destruction. The oxymoronic coffin/life buoy, pulled down to the depths by the force of the whirlpool created by Moby Dick, rises to the surface by virtue of its sealed seams and its containing "naught beneath." Ishmael also escapes the whirlpool's force because "it so chanced" that he was on "the margin of the ensuing scene." The life buoy (Queequeg's sealed coffin) and Ishmael meet and float together on a "soft and dirge-like main" until Ishmael is saved on the second day by the "devious cruising *Rachel*" looking for her lost children. The floating of the coffin/life buoy represents the oxymoronic resistance to crossing the line into the transcendent, an image marking the limits of our representative powers. The oxymoron preserves difference in its ceaseless oscillation between semantic poles as the sublime preserves the distinction between the phenomenal and noumenal realms in its ceaseless conflict between the faculties of reason and imagination. When all else succumbs to the totalitarian force of Ahab's fanaticism, the coffin/life buoy floats and serves as a support for the one who just happens to survive (528, 573).

Before the death of all but one, as the ship turns toward the equator in anticipation of the Season-on-the-Line, the crew hear a "cry so plaintively wild and unearthly—like half-articulated wailings of the ghosts of all Herod's murdered innocents." The "slaughter of the innocents" is another totalitarian act of destruction from which one escaped. The prototype for this New Testament story is in yet another totalitarian act, the slaughter of innocents following the birth of Moses. Both mass murders preceded the establishment of a new ethical order. The *Pequod,* named for the extinguished Indian tribe of New England, memorializes America's own genocidal mass murder. In the wake of the *Pequod*'s destruction comes the establishment of a new ethical order for our times. Ishmael as the prophet of this new order does not, however, identify himself with either Jesus or Moses, but with Job's messengers—those nameless witnesses who survive only to tell the story of an otherwise total destruction (428).

As we approach the apocalyptic moment in the book, the moment in which the white whale finally makes his appearance, the act of interpretation becomes more difficult, and distinguishing causes from effects, impossible. The reading of Ishmael's survival as somehow a moral vindication is for me the most difficult to sustain. If his loving relationship with Queequeg saved him, as some suggest, why did it not save Queequeg? From a moral point of view, Queequeg seems more worthy than Ishmael of being saved. What distinguishes Ishmael from all those who die? He himself admits he was one with the crew; Ahab's quest "seemed his." "Seemed" may be the key word here. Perhaps he survives because of the marginal nature of his aesthetic quest (he is after all motivated by a color—the whiteness of the whale) and the indeterminacy of his relation to the object of that quest, the white whale. Ishmael may be said to escape, in this sense, because he is an artist. Or perhaps, he is an artist, the writer of *Moby-Dick,* because he escapes. The epigraph to the epilogue, "And I only am escaped alone to tell thee," suggests a narrative necessity rather than a moral one. Without Ishmael's escape, there would be no story to tell. Ishmael's identity is subordinated to the telling of the tale.

If we are to believe the author, it is just by chance that Ishmael survives. More significant in its certainty is the survival of the oxymoronic coffin/life buoy. Ishmael would never have survived if it had not been for the *Rachel,* motivated in its "devious cruising" by love for its lost members of humanity. Ishmael is not heroic at this point, though he approaches heroic status in his quest to represent the sublimity of the whale. In the end we can only speak of one escape from telos, apocalypse, death. More significant than Ishmael's escape is the escape of Moby Dick. I think Melville's brother was right when he identified the white whale as the hero of the book. I would go one step further, naming the book itself the uncapturable.

PART II

Reading *Pierre*

6

PORTRAIT OF THE
ENTHUSIAST

WHEN MELVILLE COMPLETED *Moby-Dick*, he wrote to Hawthorne, "Leviathan is not the biggest fish in the sea, I have heard of Krackens" (143). Apparently, he was preparing to "launch his yawl" once more in quest of yet another monster. *Moby-Dick* and *Pierre* form a monstrous literary diptych that prefigures Melville's later fascination with diptychs in several of his short stories. The diptych structure helps Melville preserve difference within a totality, avoiding the totalizing tendency to reduce multiplicity to one. Melville uses diptych structures to represent economic and sexual polarization and exclusion. In "The Paradise of Bachelors and the Tartarus of Maids," for example, the juxtaposition is clearly gender-determined. The two stories suggest that the extravagant lifestyle of the bachelors is related to—even depends on—the deprivation of the excluded maids. The result is a "total" picture that could not be achieved through the presentation of only one scene from one perspective. The relationship between *Moby-Dick* and *Pierre* is similarly gender-determined. During a period characterized by rigidly separate spheres for men and women, Melville could not hope to capture a panoramic view of his world with the *Pequod* alone as his setting—no matter how many different perspectives he was able to include. Home and Mother, excluded from *Moby-Dick*, return with a vengeance in the landlocked, domestic, feminized world of *Pierre*. Through the two books, *Moby-Dick* and *Pierre*, Melville gives us a stereoscopic view of his world.

The relationship between *Moby-Dick* and *Pierre* is not limited to their respective gendered spheres of influence, however. Melville makes it clear through the conflation of images of mountains and whales in *Pierre* that he has not yet given up his quest for the sublime. He dedicates *Pierre* to Mount Greylock—the mountain that Melville faced out his window while writing both *Moby-Dick* and *Pierre* and that he thought looked "very like a whale"—calling it his "own immediate sovereign lord and king." He also names an important character in the book, Plinlimmon, after a mountain in Wales and even has Pierre pay homage to a whalelike rock. In both *Moby-Dick* and *Pierre* Melville's quest for the sublime inevitably leads to the mountains of scripture. He evokes Mount Sinai when Ishmael, at a loss to represent the face of the whale, quotes God's refusal to show his face to Moses, a refusal recalling God's commandment handed down from the mountain top forbidding image making. The Hebrew scriptures tower in *Moby-Dick;* the New Testament dominates *Pierre,* especially in the title character's encounter with what the narrator refers to as "that divine mount," the Sermon on the Mount (289).

Melville may also have had in mind a relationship between his two books modeled on the ancient diptych of Hebrew and Christian thought, the Bible. Perhaps, Melville, like Pierre, was aspiring to "gospelize the world anew" when he wrote to Hawthorne in 1851: "Though I wrote the Gospels in this century, I should die in the gutter." There is evidence to suggest that Melville saw his task in such high ethical terms. For example, he compares Shakespeare, another writer and mere mortal, to Jesus: "Ah, he's full of sermons-on-the-mount, and gentle, aye, almost as Jesus. I take such men to be inspired. I fancy that this moment Shakspeare in heaven ranks with Gabriel Raphael and Michael. And if another Messiah ever comes twill be in Shakesper's person" (*Pierre,* 273; *Letters,* 129, 77).

In "Hawthorne and His Mosses" Melville makes it clear that he does not consider the level of Shakespeare's achievement to be beyond an American writer. Writing to Duyckinck, Melville suggests that an American could reach an even greater height. If Shakespeare were alive and writing in America, he would be able to write his "full articulations" without having them "intercepted" by "that muzzle which all men wore on their souls in the Elizebethan day." Shakespeare's art, Melville suggests, was limited in its free expression by the dominant political ideology of the day. "For I hold it a verity, that even Shakspeare, was not a frank man to the uttermost. And, indeed, who in this intolerant Universe is, or can be? But the Declaration of Independence makes a difference" (*Letters*, 80). Apparently, Melville hoped to write a new gospel according to the spirit of freedom and egalitarianism that he saw expressed in the Declaration of Independence.

Whereas *Moby-Dick*, the first half of Melville's diptych, is devoted to a critique of fanaticism, *Pierre* represents a critique of enthusiasm. When Ahab collapses the difference between the world of ideas and sensible impressions by personifying all evil in the white whale, he relinquishes the possibility of his freedom from natural determinism. Because, in terms of Kant's theory, the concept of freedom cannot be demonstrated empirically, it belongs to the realm of ideas, a realm that must be outside the economy of representation. Not only does Ahab give up his own freedom in his fanaticism, but he restricts the freedom of his crew, like those governments Kant criticized for reducing their subjects to "passive beings" through positive presentations of morality. If only negative representation can begin to do justice to freedom, then Ishmael's strategies of negative representation take on political significance. The absence of all images in negative representation, however, can also pose a threat to freedom, as Kant argues in his discussion of enthusiasm. "Where the senses see nothing more before them and the indelible idea of morality remains" it then becomes necessary to "moderate the impetus of an unbounded imagination" in order to prevent it from "rising to enthusiasm" (*Judgment*, 115).

The concept of enthusiasm defined within the context of sublime aesthetics is a useful key for bringing together several thematic strands in *Pierre* concerning kinship structures and incest, music, and the hierarchical relations between social-economic classes. It can also provide insight into Melville's own relationship to this painfully introspective book. Distinguishing between the concept of enthusiasm and that of fanaticism can help define more clearly the difference between Ahab and Pierre and the relationship between *Moby-Dick* and *Pierre*. To understand the significance of the figure of "the enthusiast" in Melville's work, we need to recover meanings and contexts that are practically lost to us today. Nancy Craig Simmons has done an excellent job recovering many of these contexts for readers of *Pierre*.[1] My task is to extend her work by situating Melville's portrait of enthusiasm in the context of Kant's theory of the sublime thereby clarifying the differences between fanaticism and enthusiasm as represented in *Moby-Dick* and *Pierre*.

In the wake of the French Revolution the terms *fanaticism* and *enthusiasm* appeared in warnings against the pitfalls of reformist and idealist thought. The word *fanaticism* seems to be as popular as ever. It consistently carries negative connotations and often appears in a representational context, that is, in arguments over the meanings of words.[2] The word *enthusiasm*, on the other hand, appears to have lost most of its negative, political, and philosophical connotations. The danger of overenthusiasm usually poses no more serious threat than social embarrassment, the need for the prefix suggesting that the word has lost the negative power it had in Melville's day when its connotations were hotly debated.

It is generally assumed that *Pierre* represents Melville's vicious attack on the enthusiast. Critics are actually more likely to express sympathy with Ahab's fanaticism (in the name of Melville's darkness) than they are with Pierre's enthusiasm. If we understand the concept of enthusiasm solely in terms of religious fundamentalism, then it is indeed difficult to see how Melville would treat it sympathetically; but the meanings of the word were shifting in Melville's day. While many empiricists were writing treatises on the folly of enthusiasm, romantics embraced enthusiasm as an essential ingredient of poetry and expanded its meaning beyond the exclusively religious usage. Transcendental philosophers such as Kant tended to treat enthusiasm in a more positive light than did empiricists such as Locke (Tucker, 31).

One famous popularizer of the Kantian distinction between the fanatic and the enthusiast whose writings provide an interesting context from which to consider Melville's treatment of the enthusiast was Madame de Staël. Melville read and admired de Staël.[3] After hearing her work discussed on his ocean voyage with Adler, Melville purchased a copy of *Corinne* when he arrived in London (*Journal*, 14). *Corinne* is De Staël's own portrait of the enthusiast.[4] Like *Pierre*, it tells the story of passionate, artistic youth in conflict with social conventions. Melville may have had the figure of Corinne in mind when he created Isabel, the heroine of *Pierre*, as there are some interesting links between the two characters. Both Isabel and Corinne are dark, emotionally volatile, Latin types who are contrasted with mild blondes—Lucy in Melville's book and Lucile in de Staël's. They are also both improvisatory musicians and singers. The character of Corinne was inspired by a famous Italian "improvisatrice" named Isabel Pellegrine.[5] Although Melville's Isabel bears a striking resemblance to Corinne, the primary subject of Melville's portrait of the enthusiast is not Isabel, but Pierre, whom Isabel inspires and for whom the book is titled. *Corinne* and *Pierre* are not only portraits of enthusiasm but also in many ways self-portraits of their authors. Melville and de Staël, in their identifications with their enthusiastic heroes, are kindred spirits.

Madame de Staël wrote several essays on the subject of enthusiasm in her book *Germany*, which was published in English in New York in 1814. Melville purchased a copy in 1862 (Leyda, 647). These essays touch on many of the themes of youthful idealism and antimaterialism found in *Pierre*. It is possible that Melville read them before writing *Pierre*. My purpose in citing them, however, is not to trace a chronological line of influence, but to suggest affinities between the two authors that derive from a similar philosophical perspective. Apparently influenced by Kantian philosophy, de Staël treats the enthusiast's idealism much more positively than empiricists like Locke and Taylor, whose works Nancy Craig Simmons juxtaposes with Melville's. Madame de Staël's defense of enthusiasm gives us some indication of the philosophical and political stakes involved in the controversy surrounding the term in Melville's day. She tries to redeem the positive connotations of *enthusiasm* at a time when it was being attacked.

In her essay "The Influence of Enthusiasm on the Enlightenment" the term appears stripped of its religious connotations and situated (as fanaticism often was) in the context of revolutionary politics. Madame de Staël is concerned that the events of postrevolutionary France have left people with "souls blasé."[6] "The terrible events of which we have been witnesses have dried up men's hearts, and everything that belongs to thought appeared tarnished by the side of the omnipotence of actions." Melville marked that passage in his personal copy and also the following in which de Staël expresses a concern for young people who, "ambitious of appearing free from all enthusiasm, affect a philosophical contempt for exalted sentiments: they think by that to display a precocious force of reason; but it is a premature decay of which they are boasting. They treat talent like the old man who asked, *whether love still existed.* The mind deprived of imagination would gladly treat even nature with disdain, if nature were not too strong for it" (*Melville's Marginalia,* 664, 665). Of particular significance for our purposes is the care with which Madame de Staël distinguishes enthusiasm from fanaticism in the following passage. Melville may have had this distinction in mind when he decided to contrast the enthusiast Pierre with the fanatic/monomaniac Ahab:

> Let me repeat: enthusiasm has nothing to do with fanaticism, and cannot lead people astray. Enthusiasm is tolerant—not out of indifference, but because it makes us feel the interest and beauty of everything. Reason does not replace the happiness it takes away from us; enthusiasm finds in the heart's reverie and the mind's whole range of thought what fanaticism and passion concentrate in a single idea, a single object. The universality of this feeling is precisely what makes it favorable to thought and imagination. (de Staël, 322)

Madame de Staël devotes several chapters to enthusiasm in her book on German culture because, she says, enthusiasm is "characteristic of the quest for abstract truths which are cultivated in Germany with remarkable ardor and loyalty." Although her discussion of enthusiasm and fanaticism seems to be derived from her readings of Kant (*Germany* includes lucid essays on Kant's philosophy), in her idealist pro-German polemic to her non-German readers she shows herself to be less sensitive to the dangers of enthusiasm than her apparent source. Neither Kant nor Melville would have gone so far as to assert that enthusiasm, in contrast to fanaticism, cannot "lead people astray" (de Staël, 321, 322).

On the dangers of fanaticism, de Staël, Melville, and Kant all seem to be in agreement. They arise from the monomaniac's concentration on a "single idea, a single object" (de Staël, 322). Just as Kant insists on the incompatibility of fanaticism and the sublime, Melville, through the device of parallel quests, defines his sublime art in *Moby-Dick* ultimately against the monomania of the fanatic. On the other hand, Melville, again like Kant, treats enthusiasm with greater ambivalence.[7] Kant's definition of enthusiasm is particularly significant for our purposes because he, like Melville, explores enthusiasm in relation to fanaticism and the sublime limits to representation. Kant discusses enthusiasm when advocating the political benefits of negative representation and praising the Hebrew ban on representation in general. Enthusiasm is "the idea of the good conjoined with [strong] affection." Enthusiastic "affection" differs from fanatic "passion." Affections, like Pierre's enthusiasm, for example, are "stormy and unpremeditated" like "indignation in the form of wrath"; passions, like Ahab's fanaticism, are "steady and deliberate" like indignation "in the form of hatred (revenge)." Whereas in an affection "the freedom of the mind is *hindered,* in a passion it is *abolished.*" Therefore, according to Kant, a passion like fanaticism can never be considered sublime. On the other hand, enthusiasm "seems to be sublime, to the extent that we commonly assert that nothing great could be done without it" (*Judgment,* 112).

Melville seems to agree that enthusiasm, in contrast to fanaticism, can be seen as a sublime feeling. Melville's narrator calls Pierre's "enthusiast resolution" to "marry" Isabel, for example, a "sublime resolve." As to the "ultimate utilitarian advisability" of this resolution, "Infallibly he knows that his own voluntary steps are taking him forever from the brilliant chandeliers of the mansion of Saddle Meadows, to join company with the wretched rush-lights of poverty and woe. But his sublime intuitiveness also paints to him the sun-like glories of god-like truth and virtue; which though ever obscured by the dense fogs of earth, still shall shine eventually in unclouded radiance, casting illustrative light upon the sapphire throne of God." Pierre's "sublime intuitiveness" leads him to reject the materialism of this world, declare solidarity with the marginal and excluded of society, and follow the enthusiast's path promising "sun-like glories of god-like truth and virtue." For those accustomed to emphasizing the darkness in Melville's works, this image of sun-like truth is puzzling as we ponder Melville's relation to his rhetoric in *Pierre.* Whether Melville means for us to take this passage or anything he writes in *Pierre, or the Ambiguities* at face value is an important question for every reader of the book to consider (106, 111, 89).

Melville's first use of a third-person narrator in *Pierre* may be part of a deliberate attempt to create an ambiguous tone. One can extract almost any passage from the text and wonder endlessly whether it is meant to be read ironically, or whether Melville, through his narrator, is mocking Pierre's enthusiasm. According to Madame de Staël in her defense of enthusiasm, irony is enthusiasm's enemy, as Melville noted in his copy of her text:

Love, genius, talent, distress itself, all these sacred things are exposed to irony and it is impossible to calculate to what point the
empire of this irony may extend. There is a relish in wickedness;
there is something weak in goodness. Admiration for great things
may be made the sport of wit; and he who attaches no importance
to any thing, has the air of being superior to every thing; if, therefore, our hearts and our minds are not defended by enthusiasm,
they are exposed on all sides to be surprised by this darkest shade
of the beautiful, which unites insolence to gayety. (*Melville's Marginalia,* 664)

In *Pierre* Melville emphasizes this antagonism between irony and enthusiasm by using "earnest" synonymously with enthusiasm (see 166,
207, 264). The passage from *Pierre* evoking the "sun-like glories of god-
like truth and virtue" could be read ironically as a description of Pierre's
delusion, a belief in the triumph of light that Melville (many of us like to
think) did not share. Certainly this reading has merit. Although I do not
mean to dismiss the ironic and parodic readings of *Pierre's* enthusiastic
rhetoric, I do mean to complicate matters by suggesting that Melville
had an "earnest" attachment to this rhetoric. I hear in the book a calculated tonal tension between irony and enthusiasm/earnestness. This
oscillating undecidability of tone is the heartbeat of the text's ambiguity.
In the passage cited above, as in so many others, I think Melville means
for us to feel the pull toward the sublime in Pierre's "self-renouncing
enthusiasm," to appreciate, on an aesthetic and emotional level at least,
Pierre's "Christ-like feeling" as he attempts to "square" himself "by the
inflexible rule of holy right" (205, 106).

Kant explains the ambivalence many feel toward enthusiasm as a conflict between aesthetic sensibility and rationality. The enthusiast's state
of mind seems sublime, he writes, because we commonly assert that
"nothing great can be done without it." But an "absence of affection" in
a mind that "vigorously follows its unalterable principles" is, for Kant,
more sublime than enthusiasm, because it has on its side the "satisfaction of pure reason." Enthusiasm as a "blind" affection can never win
the approval of reason. Melville may have known this intellectually, but
he had too much of the romantic in him to accept it without protest.
Kant was no romantic; he was, however, a transcendentalist and, as
such, was willing to grant that on an *aesthetic* level prior to cognition

enthusiasm does have something sublime about it "because it is a tension of forces produced by ideas, which give an impulse to the mind that operates far more powerfully and lastingly than the impulse arising from sensible representations" (*Judgment*, 112–13).

In contrast to critiques of enthusiasm from an empirical perspective, Melville's treatment of the enthusiast plays on Kant's different levels of aesthetic attraction and rational repulsion. Later in life, Melville wrote a poem called "The Enthusiast" in which he returns to many of the same images and themes he explored in *Pierre*, with, I would argue, equal ambivalence:

> "Though He slay me yet will I trust in Him."
>
> Shall hearts that beat no base retreat
>   In youth's magnanimous years—
> Ignoble hold it, if discreet
>   When interest tames to fears;
> Shall spirits that worship light
>   Perfidious deem its sacred glow,
>   Recant, and trudge where worldings go,
> Conform and own them right?
>
> Shall Time with creeping influence cold
>   Unnerve and cow? the heart
> Pine for the heartless ones enrolled
>   With palterers of the mart?
> Shall faith abjure her skies,
>   Or pale probation blench her down
>   To shrink from Truth so still, so lone
> Mid loud gregarious lies?
>
> Each burning boat in Caesar's rear,
>   Flames—No return through me!
> So put the torch to ties though dear,
>   If ties but tempters be.
> Nor cringe if come the night:
>   Walk through the cloud to meet the pall,
>   Though light forsake thee, never fall
> From fealty to light.

It is misleading to read this poem as simply a "highly derogatory ... epithet derisive of zealots and fanatical devotion," as William Bysshe Stein has done (84). Stein collapses the distinction between fanaticism and enthusiasm and goes too far in disassociating Melville from the latter.[8] When Stein writes that the poem is about the "unwisdom of youth ... the age of ignorance, of service to dream and wishful thinking," he astutely recognizes in the poem the same youthful "world of Pierre"; but he overlooks Melville's own attachment to the enthusiast's rhetoric (85). The questions asked in the first two stanzas were questions that Melville never tired of asking. We have only to recall his motto that he kept within eyesight on his writing desk, "Be true to the dreams of your youth," and his epigraph from Hawthorne that he used for the title page of *Weeds and Wildings:* "Youth is the proper, permanent, and genuine condition of man" (*Collected Poems*, 299).

The definition in the poem of truth "so still, so lone" is one with which Melville could sympathize. The last stanza of the poem, in which the enthusiast expresses a desire "to put the torch to ties though dear, / If ties but tempters be," need not be read as the expression of the enthusiast disowning "the Christian brotherhood of love" (Stein, 86). It is true that Melville is critical of Ahab's fanatical disregard for all human ties, but he treats Pierre's enthusiastic renunciation of his familial ties with ambivalence within a Christian context. In "The Enthusiast to Duty" he writes, "the heaven-begotten Christ is born; and will not own a mortal parent, and spurns and rends all mortal bonds" (*Pierre*, 106).

Melville's ambivalent treatment of enthusiasm in *Pierre* corresponds to his own ambivalent feelings about Christianity. Pierre's conflict centers around his encounter with a text Melville admired, a text that the narrator calls "the greatest real miracle of all religions, the Sermon on the Mount." The egalitarian message of the Sermon, its expressions of solidarity with the marginalized and lowly, speaks powerfully to Pierre. Although attracted on an aesthetic level to "the beauty of chronometrical excellence, [which] that divine mount" represents, the enthusiast faces a painful dilemma when he tries to reconcile those "sentences which embody all the love of the Past, and all the love which can be imagined in any conceivable Future," with the "downright positive falsity" of a "mammonish" world "saturated and soaking with lies." This is the conflict Plinlimmon outlines in his pamphlet, the hard truth the enthusiast Pierre has to face. "Hereupon then in the soul of the enthusiast youth, two armies come to shock; and unless he prove recreant, or unless he prove gullible, or unless he can find the talismanic secret, to reconcile this world with his own soul, then there is no peace for him, no slightest truce for him in this life. Now without doubt this Talismanic Secret has never yet been found; and in the nature of human things it seems as though it never can be" (207, 215, 207, 290).

If we compare that passage with Hawthorne's description of Melville written after their 1857 meeting in Liverpool, we can see that at least one person recognized the same "enthusiastic" quality in Melville:

> Melville, as he always does, began to reason of Providence and futurity, and of everything that lies beyond human ken, and informed me that he had "pretty much made up his mind to be annihilated"; but still he does not seem to rest in that anticipation; and, I think, will never rest until he gets hold of a definite belief. It is strange how he persists—and has persisted ever since I knew him, and probably long before—in wandering to and fro over these deserts, as dismal and monotonous as the sand hills amid which we were sitting. He can neither believe, nor be comfortable in his unbelief; and he is too honest and courageous not to try to do one or the other. If he were a religious man, he would be one of the most truly religious and reverential; he has a very high and noble nature, and better worth immortality than most of us. (cited in Leyda, 529)

For Melville, as for the enthusiast, there was no peace, no truce in this life. He could not prove "recreant" or "gullible" and he knew the search for the "talismanic secret" that would "reconcile this world with his soul" was in vain. Melville's enthusiasm is tempered by a sober refusal to cross over the line into the transcendent like "Plato, and Spinoza, and Goethe" and the "preposterous rabble of Muggletonian Scots and Yankees, whose vile brogue still the more bestreaks the stripedness of their Greek or German Neoplatonical originals" (*Pierre*, 208). Melville's brand of transcendentalism, like Kant's, entails a critical respect for limits, such as the limits of representation separating the noumena from the phenomena.

A discussion of Melville's portrait of enthusiasm in *Pierre* must take some account of Melville's identification with Pierre. Melville seems to be inviting us to do just that by packing the text with obvious autobiographical references. If we compare *Moby-Dick* in this regard, we find the autobiographical references limited primarily to Ishmael: like Melville, Ishmael had worked as a merchant marine, a school teacher, and a whaler and wrote a book of his experiences. These references, along with the device of the parallel quests, serve to distance Melville from Ahab's fanaticism. Not so in *Pierre* where the main mediating devices separating Melville from Pierre's enthusiasm are an "objective" analytic third-person narrator and a painfully ambiguous and ironic tone.

For evidence of Melville's close attachment to the enthusiast's rhetoric, we have only to look to his letters to Hawthorne. Here he openly declares his allegiance: "I stand for the heart. To the dogs with the head!" (129). Just so Pierre cries, "The heart! the heart! 'tis God's anointed; let me pursue the heart!" (91). In his letters to Hawthorne especially, Melville gives his heart full rein and speaks in language surprisingly like that of *Pierre*. He writes of feeling "pantheistic" when he first learned that Hawthorne had read *Moby-Dick*. He says, "your heart beat in my ribs and mine in yours, and both in God's." Hawthorne may have lived in a commune, but I doubt he was prepared for the intimacy of Melville's imagery in the following passages: "Whence come you, Hawthorne? By what right do you drink from my flagon of life? And when I put it to my lips—lo, they are yours and not mine. I feel that the Godhead is broken up like the bread at the Supper, and that we are the pieces. Hence this infinite fraternity of feeling" (142).

In response to what was possibly Hawthorne's weak praise for *Moby-Dick* (Hawthorne's letter is unfortunately missing), Melville evinces an enthusiastic, Pierre-like "faith in ye Invisibles" when he valorizes the idea behind the written word (*Pierre*, 107). "Now, sympathizing with the paper, my angel turns over another page. You did not care a penny for the book. But, now and then as you read, you understood the pervading thought that impelled the book—and that you praised. Was it not so? You were archangel enough to despise the imperfect body, and embrace the soul. Once you hugged the ugly Socrates because you saw the flame in the mouth, and heard the rushing of the demon,—the familiar,—and recognized the sound; for you have heard it in your own solitudes." This letter represents the peak of Melville's enthusiastic expression. It is also, as Davis and Gilman point out in their edition of Melville's letters (on page 142), the one time, except in letters to family members, that Melville signs only his first name. Hereafter, his correspondence to Hawthorne becomes cooler and less frequent. Perhaps the homoerotic implications in Melville's images of hugging Socrates and of fusing lips and ribs proved too much for Hawthorne. The cooling off of their relationship coincided significantly with the writing of *Pierre*. Melville, in a letter to Hawthorne's wife (which contains the first mention of *Pierre*), may be identifying himself with his new hero when he chooses for the first and only time to close his letter with "Earnestly Thine" (*Letters*, 142, 147).

Although there is no need to go so far as to collapse the difference between Melville and Pierre, it is important to see this level of Melville's engagement with his enthusiastic hero. In *Pierre* Melville focuses on an aspect of himself of which he was painfully aware and not at liberty to exorcise. He isolates enthusiasm and extends it to its logical and dangerous limits. The letters Melville wrote to Hawthorne touch on these "danger" zones. The surfacing of homoerotic imagery, for example, corresponds in *Pierre* to the hero's entanglement with the incest taboo. Enthusiasm, for both Melville and Pierre, opposes social convention. "With no son of man do I stand upon any etiquette or ceremony, except the Christian ones of charity and honesty," Melville writes in an early letter to Hawthorne. In his enthusiasm for democracy Melville extends the Christian egalitarian values expressed in the Sermon on the Mount to the social and political realm. Melville is a radical democrat in his letters espousing a belief in an "unconditional democracy in all things"—a "ruthless democracy" that "boldly declares that a thief in jail is as honorable a personage as Gen. George Washington." In *Pierre* he turns his title character into such a democrat, admitting that he may be a little "too radical" for the readers' taste (*Pierre*, 13). Although Melville acknowledges in his letter that what he is saying is "ludicrous," he writes, "Truth is the silliest thing under the sun. Try to get a living by the Truth—and go to the Soup Societies. . . . All Reformers, are bottomed upon the truth, more or less; and to the world at large are not reformers almost universally laughingstocks? Why so? Truth is ridiculous to men." The impetus for political change lies in the enthusiast's utopian vision. Melville seems to recognize the need for enthusiasm, even while he paints a rather bleak picture of the possibilities for change (*Letters*, 126, 127).

In *Pierre* the ideology of radical democracy behind the enthusiast's rejection of the status quo entails an antihierarchical leveling of human relationships that can lead to transgression of social taboos. Pierre's indifference to conventional ties can be seen, for example, in his practice of calling his mother "sister." Their relationship, writes Melville, "seemed almost to realize here below the sweet dreams of the religious enthusiasts, who paint for us a Paradise to come, when etherealized from all drosses and stains, the holiest passion of man shall unite all kindreds and climes in one circle of pure and unimpairable delight." When Pierre has to face the possibility of introducing his mother to his new-found "sister" Isabel, he knows that his mother is too conventional to ever accept this relationship. His "enthusiastic heart sunk in and in, and caved away in him, as he so poignantly felt his first feeling of the dreary heart-vacancies of the conventional life." His eventual resolve to "marry" Isabel, to "sacrifice all objects dearest to him, and cut himself away from his last hopes of common happiness" will prove, says the narrator, "how gossamer, and thinner and more impalpable than airiest threads of gauze . . . all common conventional regardings" were to Pierre. Pierre the enthusiast "spurns and rends all mortal bonds" according to Christ's teaching: "And every one that hath forsaken houses, or brethren, or sisters, or father, or mother, or wife, or children, or lands, for my name's sake, shall receive an hundredfold, and shall inherit everlasting life" (16, 106; Matt. 19:29). Deep inside himself Pierre felt "a divine unidentifiableness, that owned no earthly kith or kin" (89).[9]

Pierre's enthusiastic "unidentifiableness" translates on a logical and discursive level into a fear of "tautology," the positing of identity. The dread of tautology, writes Melville, is the "continual torment of some earnest minds, and, as such, is surely a weakness in them." Although pronouncing such dread a weakness, Melville, in his characteristic ambivalence toward enthusiasm, considers the case of Virgil: "no wise man will wonder at conscientious Virgil all eager at death to burn his *Aeneid* for a monstrous heap of inefficient superfluity." The enthusiast's dread of tautology is linked in this passage to the artist's deepest utilitarian fears of the inadequacy of his or her creation. It may be a weakness, but not to dread tautology, continues the narrator, "only belongs to those enviable dunces, whom the partial God hath blessed, over all the earth, with the inexhaustible self-riches of vanity, and folly, and a blind self-complacency" (277).

The enthusiast's unidentifiableness and consequent fear of tautology corresponds in the book to distrust of the unifying function of representation. In contrast to fanatics, who brashly try to represent that which cannot be represented, enthusiasts are painfully aware of the limits of their powers of representation. The enthusiast, according to the narrator, lacks that "all-comprehending oneness, that calm representativeness, by which a steady philosophic mind reaches forth and draws to itself, in their collective entirety, the objects of its contemplations." By the enthusiast's "eagerness, all objects are deceptively foreshortened; by his intensity each object is viewed as detached; so that essentially and relatively everything is misseen by him" (175). Stripped of their determining ties to one another, all objects are leveled in the enthusiast's mind, just as Pierre levels social hierarchies and human relationships. This breaking of ties leads, as it did in *Moby-Dick,* to an exploration of the limits to our powers of representation.

Pierre comes up against those limits in his encounter with Isabel and his hopeless entanglement with the incest taboo. By "marrying" Isabel, Pierre breaks all conventional ties and finds himself tied to one who has no reference. Isabel's socioeconomic status as an orphaned woman and member of the impoverished servant class is marginal. Because Isabel lies outside the economy of representation, Pierre lacks any "evidence" by which to determine whether the woman he has taken for his "bride" is his sister. Pierre's enthusiastic embrace of the "Invisibles" has led him right into the heart of ambiguity (107).

7

ISABEL AND THE VALORIZATION OF MUSIC

PIERRE'S ENTHUSIASM FOR that which lies beyond representation is figured in his devotion to the marginalized Isabel. In presenting Isabel as a musician, Melville introduces an aesthetic dimension to this character's "unrepresentedness." On this aesthetic level, Isabel functions as a figure for the nonrepresentational art of music. The story of Pierre, Isabel, and Lucy reads as an allegory of the relations between the arts, with Lucy representing the visual, Isabel, the musical, and Pierre, the literary arts. The poet Pierre's devotion to Isabel the musician allegorizes a valorization of the nonrepresentational art of music by the literary artist. In return for Pierre's devotion, Isabel bestows on him "blessings that are imageless to all mortal fancyings." "Not mere sounds of common words," she tells him, "but inmost tones of my heart's deepest melodies should now be audible to thee." When Isabel sings and plays her guitar, Pierre responds by valorizing music over language: "Any,—all words are thine, words and worlds with all their containings shall be slaves to thee." "For where the deepest words end," the narrator tells us, "there music begins with its supersensuous and all-confounding intimations" (114, 113, 313, 282).

This allegory of the arts in *Pierre* tells a familiar tale in the history of aesthetics—that of music's ascendance in the late eighteenth and nineteenth centuries to the top of the hierarchy of the arts, where her exemplary status as a nonrepresentational art form frees her sister arts from the constraints of mimesis. Wherever the "lamp" replaced the "mirror" as a symbol of artistic production, there music was extolled as a model for the other arts.[1] Poe, Baudelaire, Mallarmé, Valéry, Whistler, Schopenhauer, Nietzsche, and Pater are some of the artists, philosophers, and critics inspired by the example of music as they challenged representational models of the arts. Walter Pater went so far as to proclaim in 1873 that "all art constantly aspires to the condition of music" (95). When many were feeling threatened by increasing realism and positivism, the nonrepresentational art of music served as a refuge for those interested in exploring the limits of representation. Although *Pierre*'s valorization of music needs to be situated within this historical context, it also needs to be distinguished from the tradition by Melville's addition of a political dimension usually missing from the more narrowly focused aestheticism. The nonrepresentational art of music in *Pierre* functions as an aesthetic analogue to Isabel's political unrepresentedness, that is, her marginal status in the socioeconomic power structure.

Philosophically, the valorization of music in nineteenth-century aesthetics is linked to the exploration of the limits to our powers of representation begun by Kant with his critique of reason and theory of the sublime. A direct line of influence leads from Kant's philosophy to the valorization of music found in the influential works of Schopenhauer and in Nietzsche's *Birth of Tragedy*.[2] Though Melville could not have read Nietzsche's *Birth of Tragedy* when he wrote *Pierre,* and he only later became an avid reader of Schopenhauer, his affinities with this philosophical tradition are striking and worth investigating.

For many artists and thinkers, music comes to "represent" paradoxically that which stands outside of representation. Music has a sublime aspect. Elizabeth McKinsey, in her history of the artistic attempts to represent the sublimity of Niagara Falls, notes a shift in nineteenth-century writings on the falls toward aural and musical metaphors. Margaret Fuller, for example, heard the Music of the Spheres echoed in the falls. Composer Eugene M. Thayer, who attempted to "record the harmonies and rhythms created by the Falls in standard musical notation," concluded that it is "the sublimist music on earth" (cited in McKinsey, 218–19). Through the figure of Isabel in *Pierre,* Melville links standard imagery of the sublime with the power of music. Lucy evokes the composer whose music exemplified the sublime when she associates Isabel's face with "wild Beethoven sounds" (54). Isabel triggers an agitation in Pierre's soul that is much like the experience of the sublime as Kant had determined it. Like Kant, Melville takes care in this passage from *Pierre* to avoid the empirical trap of locating the sublime in the object. The sublime state of mind indicates the infinite capacity of the human soul:

> From without no wonderful effect is wrought within ourselves, unless some interior, responding wonder meets it. That the starry vault shall surcharge the heart with all rapturous marvelings, is only because we ourselves are greater miracles, and superber trophies than all the stars in universal space. Wonder interlocks with wonder; and then the confounding feeling comes. No cause have we to fancy, that a horse, a dog, a fowl, ever stand transfixed beneath yon skyey load of majesty. But our soul's arches underfit into its; and so, prevent the upper arch from falling on us with unsustainable inscrutableness. 'Explain ye my deeper mystery,' said the shepherd Chaldean king, smiting his breast, lying on his back upon the plain; 'and then, I will bestow all my wonderings upon ye, ye stately stars!' So, in some sort, with Pierre. Explain thou this strange integral feeling in me myself, he thought—turning upon the fancied face—and I will then renounce all other wonders, to gaze wonderingly at thee. But thou hast evoked in me profounder spells than the evoking one, thou face! For me, thou hast uncovered one infinite, dumb, beseeching countenance of mystery, underlying all the surfaces of visible time and space. (51–52)

Here Kant's experience of the sublime is triggered, not by "nature," but by the face of another. Pierre's encounter with Isabel triggers an expansion of the soul in which his mind is opened to the limits of representation, to that which lies beyond the "surfaces of visible time and space." Along with this insight into the limits of representation, however, comes a tragic sense as Isabel introduces Pierre to the "darker, though truer aspect of things." After this impoverished, orphaned woman enters his life, Pierre can see the "infinite cliffs and gulfs of human mystery and misery [in the] sublime Italian, Dante" (68, 54).

In moving from Kant's theory of the sublime to the valorization of music and tragedy, we move beyond Kant as such and into the implications worked out by his successors. The same configuration of tragedy, music, and the sublime in *Pierre* can be found, for example, in Nietzsche's *Birth of Tragedy from the Spirit of Music*. Both Nietzsche and Melville explore the limits to our powers of representation and the implications such limits have for theories of art. Both authors work within an aesthetic tradition that owes a great deal to Kant's philosophical revolution. Nietzsche acknowledges his debt to both Kant and Schopenhauer (whose extension of Kant's philosophical system entailed a valorization of music) when he praises the way these philosophers have used

> science itself to point out the limits and the relativity of knowledge generally, and thus to deny decisively the claim of science to universal validity and universal aims. And their demonstration diagnosed for the first time the illusory notion which pretends to be able to fathom the innermost essence of things with the aid of causality. The extraordinary courage and wisdom of *Kant* and *Schopenhauer* have succeeded in gaining the most difficult victory, the victory over the optimism concealed in the essence of logic— an optimism that is the basis of our culture. . . . With this insight a culture is inaugurated that I venture to call a tragic culture. (112)

According to Nietzsche, the discoveries of Kant and Schopenhauer have made it possible for the "spirit of German philosophy" to "destroy scientific Socratism's complacent delight in existence by establishing its boundaries." Out of this destruction, writes Nietzsche, comes "an infinitely profounder and more serious view of ethical problems and of art, which we may designate as Dionysian wisdom comprised in concepts." Furthermore, the insight into the limitations of the scientific empirical method provided by Kant and Schopenhauer is intimately linked, according to Nietzsche, with the increasing realization of music's power. Nietzsche sees a "oneness of German music and philosophy." Along with the revolutionary power of German philosophy, "another power has arisen, from Bach to Beethoven, from Beethoven to Wagner, [a power that] can neither be explained nor excused [by] the primitive conditions of Socratic culture, [but that is] rather felt by this culture as something terribly inexplicable and overwhelmingly hostile." In this unity of German music and philosophy, Nietzsche envisions the "*awakening of the*

Dionysian spirit in the modern world!" because both have furnished revolutionary insights into the limits to our powers of representation (120–21, 119).

Nietzsche's familiar exposition of the Dionysian and the Apollonian drives in art is in many respects analogous to Kant's formulation of the sublime and the beautiful. Apollo, as the god of the beautiful, "exacts measure from his disciples." The ethical imperative "Nothing in excess" is conjoined with the "aesthetic necessity for beauty." Dionysus, as a god of the sublime, is Titanic and pre- or extra-Apollonian. The mysterious union of the Dionysian and Apollonian, according to Nietzsche, gave birth to the "sublime" art of tragedy. Nietzsche wrote *The Birth of Tragedy* under the direct influence of Schopenhauer who, borrowing Kantian terminology, compared music to the unrepresentable "thing-in-itself," or noumenal world, contrasting it with the phenomenal world as represented by the visual arts. It was Henry Murray in his introduction to *Pierre* who first touched on the aesthetic allegory in Melville's book when he noted the affinities between Nietzsche's Apollonian-Dionysian antithesis and the roles of Isabel and Lucy (Nietzsche, 46, 47; Murray, liii).[3]

Attention to this allegorical level of Melville's text should help mitigate some of the critical attacks on Melville's "stereotypical" portrayals of these two female characters. Admittedly, Lucy and Isabel are drawn as types. Critics picking up on the typological quality of *Pierre*'s allegory have often interpreted Lucy and Isabel in moral terms. Lucy, perhaps because she is sweet, blond, and middle class, appears to be Pierre's good angel, while the dark, mysterious Isabel is associated with the forces of darkness and evil and is blamed for Pierre's disastrous downfall. A more fruitful reading emerges if we move beyond such personifications of good and evil to see the characters as aesthetic, rather than moral, types. As a figure for the visual arts, Lucy, her name signifying light, lives, like Nietzsche's Apollo, in the world of appearance, the phenomenal world in which all is revealed to the eyes through the plastic arts. Lucy wants Pierre to be "wholly a disclosed secret" to her. The secret she needs revealed, however, is the riddle of the face that has haunted her at night with "wild Beethoven sounds": Isabel's face. Isabel, as her name suggests, is a figure for music, her marginal social status reflected in music's status on the margins of representation. Isabel's function is analogous to Ishmael's in *Moby-Dick,* with her typological status embodying the limits to typology. Like Ishmael, and also Pip, Isabel is said to be a "castaway." As a figure of marginality, Isabel paradoxically represents that which is excluded from representation (37, 54, 66).

Lucy knows that her marriage with Pierre can never happen until the riddle of Isabel's mysterious face is solved; but the riddle has no solution because Isabel represents "one infinite dumb, beseeching countenance of mystery, underlying all the surfaces of visible time and space." In Nietzschean terms Isabel brings to Pierre Dionysian wisdom. Through Isabel, Pierre learns "that this world has a secret deeper than beauty and Life some burdens heavier than death." When Isabel enters his life, Pierre has "a vague revelation [that] the visible world, some of which before had seemed but too common and prosaic to him; and but too intelligible; he now vaguely felt, that all the world and every misconceivedly common and prosaic thing in it, was steeped a million fathoms in a mysteriousness wholly hopeless of solution." Isabel's appearance triggers a turning point in Pierre's life, a shift that Melville describes using terms that suggest a crisis of representation. Isabel has the effect of tearing open the closed circle of significance that had characterized Pierre's state (52, 7, 180).

Before meeting Isabel, Pierre lived in a continuous chain of self-reference. His "very horizon," we learn, was "as a memorial ring," in which the "beautiful country round about Pierre [seemed] sanctified [through the] long uninterrupted possession by his race." The landscape was touched with a "talisman" — the "fond ideality" with which Pierre remembered his deceased father. Pierre and his mother are said to revolve in an "orbit of joy." It is the idealized memory of his father (and the economic shelter he provided) that allows the circle to remain closed and unbroken. But even before the appearance of Isabel, Pierre becomes aware of a tiny crack in the closure when he tries to account for the difference between two portraits painted at different times in his father's life. The youthful portrait done before his marriage to Pierre's mother seems to urge Pierre to "Probe, probe a little — see — there seems one little crack there, Pierre — a wedge, a wedge." This "ghost" of Pierre's father presses him to reconcile the older and younger portraits: "Consider in thy mind, Pierre, whether we two paintings may not make only one." The younger portrait tells Pierre, "In youth we *are,* but in age we seem; [we] abdicate ourselves, and take unto us another self, Pierre." In spite of the discrepancy resulting from the passage of time, Pierre still clings to his ideal image of his father—until he meets Isabel (8, 84, 83).

Isabel first appears in the book as a sound, an "unearthly, girlish shriek." This shriek "seemed to split its way clean through [Pierre's] heart, and leave a yawning gap there." Isabel's letter to Pierre triggers an explosion in Pierre's life in which "all mysteries ripped open as if with a keen sword, and forth trooped thickening phantoms of an infinite gloom." After reading Isabel's claim to be his long-lost half sister, Pierre has a mystical experience in which he joins together the "inexplicably mysterious" chair portrait of his father and the "inexplicably familiar" face of Isabel (45, 85). Isabel, as a figure for what lies beyond representation, has the power to melt solidities, erase boundaries, and break open Pierre's closed circle of significance to reveal an irreducible multiplicity and tragic ambivalence that is reflected in his reading of Dante:

> On all sides, the physical world of solid objects now slidingly displaced itself from around him, and he floated into an ether of visions; and, starting to his feet with clenched hands and outstaring eyes at the transfixed face in the air, he ejaculated that wonderful verse from Dante, descriptive of the two mutually absorbing shapes in the Inferno:
> Ah! how dost thou change, Agnello! See! thou
> art not double now, Nor only one! (85)

Isabel's music and the mysterious story of her life cause Pierre to break open that closed circle of significance and renounce all the former ties that bound him within it. He then ties himself to one who has no ties to speak of.

"I never knew a mortal mother," Isabel's story begins, and "I seem not of woman born." She calls her guitar her mother. In contrast to Pierre, whose landscape speaks continually to him of his paternity, Isabel has no idea where she was born. Like the nonrepresentational art of music, Isabel lacks reference. Her Bildungsroman tells of an existence at the margins of representation. With no one to relate to, she has lived a life of neglect and abuse. Her earliest memory is of a house as "dumb as death." "No name; no scrawled or written thing; no book, was in the house; no one memorial speaking of its former occupants." She lived with an old man and woman, who, because they never spoke to her, were indistinguishable from the house cat. Her next home is presumably an insane asylum. After spending several years there, she is hired out to work in a farmhouse where she experiences her first moment of self-consciousness when an infant smiles at her. "This beautiful infant," she tells Pierre, "first brought me to my own mind, as it were; first made me sensible that I was something different from stones, trees, cats." She envied the child at its mother's breast. The infant "saved" her, she tells Pierre, but it also gave her "vague desirings." She began to reflect in her mind, to try to recall the past, "but try as I would, little could I recall, but the bewilderingness;—and the stupor, and the torpor, and the blankness, and the dimness, and the vacant whirlingness of the bewilderingness." Through her experience with the infant and the self-consciousness she gains through her labor, Isabel gradually develops a sense of her humanness. "Now I began to feel strange differences." She sees a snake darting through the grass and says to herself, "That thing is not human, but I am human" (114, 115, 116, 122).

She then tells of a man that visited her and once whispered the word "father" in her ear. When she learns of his death, she also learns that he had been subsidizing her stay at the house and that she has to move again. At her new workplace-home, she saves enough wages to buy a guitar. At this point in her narrative, Isabel stops talking to play her music for Pierre. "Now listen to the guitar; and the guitar shall sing to thee the sequel of my story; for not in words can it be spoken." Melville, when faced with the task of representing the effect of Isabel's music, has recourse again to the figure of the oxymoron, which he uses in *Moby-Dick* to mark the limits to his powers of representation. Pierre is said to be overwhelmed by "the utter unintelligibleness, but the infinite significances of the sounds of the guitar." When they meet the next night, Pierre hears of how Isabel learned to read the name "Glendinning" from a handkerchief her father left. She never produces this important bit of evidence, nor does the enthusiast Pierre ever request to see it, but she does show him the name "Isabel" engraved inside her guitar. The seller of the guitar told her it came from the Glendinning house so it must have belonged, she concludes, to her mother, for whom Isabel believes she is named. Her story then breaks off again with a musical interlude as she whispers "Mother—mother—mother!" to the guitar and the guitar strings reverberate in sympathetic response. Pierre is "almost deprived of consciousness" when she reprieves her song from the previous night, "Mystery of Isabel" (124, 125, 126, 150).

The prose style Melville uses to describe Isabel's music and Pierre's response to it has been subject to ridicule ever since the book first appeared on the market. Not much has changed since *Godey's Lady's Book* printed their review including a parody of Melville's style:

> Under the supposition that [satire] has been his intention, we submit the following notice of his book, as the very best off-hand effort we could make in imitation of his style: . . . we have listened to its outbreathing of sweet-swarming sounds, and their melodious, mournful, wonderful, and unintelligible melodiousness has "dropped like pendulous, glittering icicles," with soft-ringing silveriness, upon our never-to-be-delighted-sufficiently organs of hearing; and, in the insignificant significancies of that deftly-stealing and wonderfully-serpentining melodiousness, we have found an infinite, unbounded, inexpressible mysteriousness of nothingness." (Leyda, 462)

It does seem odd that with all the thematic emphasis placed on music in *Pierre,* the book presents Melville the stylist at his most unmusical. If there is a method to what many see as Melville's madness in writing *Pierre,* perhaps it lies in the creation of a rift between the idea of music as represented by Isabel and the awkward unmusicality of the words used to describe that music. Melville will often coin words in *Pierre* using a method that seems more German at times than English: he turns adjectives and adverbs into substantives with the rather unmusical addition of the suffix "-ness," as in, for example, the word "mysteriousness." The result is to contrast the fluidity of music with the petrifying quality of words. Language's tendency to "petrify" is also suggested in the poet Pierre's name. By resisting the temptation to "imitate" music through language, Melville exaggerates the gap between the two and marks the limit to representation. In a similar vein Nietzsche writes:

> Language can never adequately render the cosmic symbolism of music, because music stands in symbolic relation to the primordial contradiction and primordial pain in the heart of the primal unity, and therefore symbolizes a sphere which is beyond and prior to all

phenomena. Rather, all phenomena, compared with it, are merely symbols: hence *language,* as the organ and symbol of phenomena, can never by any means disclose the innermost heart of music; language, in its attempt to imitate it, can only be in superficial contact with music; while all the eloquence of lyric poetry cannot bring the deepest significance of the latter one step nearer to us. (55–56)

Musicality of language is not an end in itself for Melville, but is generally presented in a specific context. This is another sense in which Melville's aesthetic is to be distinguished from a pure aestheticism. In *Billy Budd,* for example, the rather unmusical prose of the narrative and the Naval Gazette contrasts sharply with the mellifluous beauty of the final sailors' ballad. I find the scenes in which Isabel plays her music for Pierre to be quite moving, but not because of the beauty of Melville's prose. The tension created by the words' failure to capture a music I can barely imagine underscores for me the eroticism of the scenes and the sense of danger and risk involved in crossing class and familial boundaries. The "inadequacy" of the language functions negatively to represent that which is beyond representation. The words skim the surface of the text as the passions burn beneath.

Again, Melville marks the limits to representation with the oxymoron when Pierre, returning from his second encounter with Isabel, begins to read from *Hamlet:*

The intensest light of reason and revelation combined, cannot shed such blazonings upon the deeper truths in man, as will sometimes proceed from his own profoundest gloom. Utter darkness is then his light, and cat-like he distinctly sees all objects through a medium which is mere blindness to common vision. Wherefore have Gloom and Grief been celebrated of old as the selectest chamberlains to knowledge? Wherefore is it, that not to know Gloom and Grief is not to know aught that an heroic man should learn?

By the light of that gloom, Pierre now turned over the soul of Hamlet in his hand. (169)

With his eyes opened by the light of gloom, Pierre begins to read anew. Like his literary brother, Hamlet, whose impatience with "words, words, words" (2.1.155) illustrates the young enthusiast's impatience with the deceptive quality of representation in general, Pierre, with his new insight into the limits of representation provided by Isabel's narrative and her music, rejects the image as inadequate—particularly representations of his father—and launches a titanic assault on the world of "seeming." "Never more," he cries, "will I play the vile pigmy, and by small memorials after death, attempt to reverse the decree of death, by essaying the poor perpetuating image of the original. Let all die, and mix again!" He burns his father's chair portrait, for "how can lifelessness be fit memorial to life?" He also burns family letters and "miscellaneous memorials in paper," crying, "henceforth, cast-out Pierre hath no paternity, and no past; and since the Future is one blank to all; therefore, twice-disinherited Pierre stands untrammelledly his ever-present self!—free to do his own self-will and present fancy to whatever end!" (197–98, 199).

Like Hamlet, who evokes the myth of Enceladus when he becomes disgusted by Laertes' feeble attempts to "outface" him at the grave of Ophelia, Pierre, in launching his attack on the world of seeming, imagines himself the Titan, Enceladus, the offspring of the incestuous marriage of two worlds, heaven and earth, forever beaten down by the Olympians who bury him alive.[4] For Hamlet and Pierre, the crisis of representation centers primarily around the world of the father and the patriarchal social structure that seeks to perpetuate itself through words and images. Both texts focus on imagery of portraiture as both heroes probe beneath the deceptive surfaces of appearance. Hamlet asks Laertes, "was your father dear to you? Or are you like the painting of a sorrow, A face without a heart" (4.7.106). Pierre reads in his copy of *Hamlet,* "The time is out of joint, / Oh cursed spite, / That ever I was born to set it right" (235). Melville appears to be drawing on the imagery of framing in *Hamlet* to denote Pierre's crisis of representation. The two portraits that Hamlet holds up to the "seeming virtuous queen" of his "Hyperion" father and "Satyr" uncle (3.4), illustrate for Hamlet a political and moral disjuncture. Pierre uncovers a similar disjuncture, but Melville avoids the melodramatic personifications of good and evil and makes the attack on the patriarchal structure more pointed by locating the disjuncture within the same man: the Hyperion and Satyr are found in the two portraits of Pierre's father.

Isabel's status as an illegitimate, orphaned, impoverished woman in a patriarchal society situates her on the margins or frame of representation. When Pierre attempts to reconcile "four impossible adjuncts" by "marrying" Isabel he finds himself also living a marginal existence in an abandoned church in the company of indigent artists, scholars, and Kantian philosophers. At the margins of the structures of representation and patriarchy, Pierre becomes entangled in the incest taboo. Melville is uncompromising in his representation of this state of marginality. If Isabel is truly marginal in terms of the structures of representation and patriarchy, then we can never really know if she is Pierre's sister or not. Here we find the central ambiguity of the book. Pierre was drawn to Isabel on the basis of her resemblance to the chair portrait of Pierre's father. When near the end he finds another portrait she resembles— a portrait of a stranger, the question arises whether it is ever possible to break out of the economy of resemblance and representation to get at some "truth" beneath the surface. In his youthful enthusiasm Pierre has begun to "see through the first superficiality of the world" and "he fondly weens he has come to the unlayered substance." But, the narrator reminds us, "far as any geologist has yet gone down into the world, it is found to consist of nothing but surface stratified on surface" (285).

Although Isabel's music takes Pierre to the limits of representation, there is no crossing over. Pierre first encounters those limits as an expansion of the soul, but in the end he remains a "states-prisoner of letters" (340). For the youthful enthusiast Pierre, this insight proves too painful to bear. Still, the insight provided by music into the limits of representation clears a path for a critique of the representational methods by which those in power retain their control. The writings of Ernst Bloch can help us to bring the valorization of music in *Pierre* out of the realm of pure aestheticism and into a political context. For Bloch, music is the "most utopian of the arts." In "social terms," music is "seismographic, it reflects cracks under the social surface, expresses wishes for change, bids us to hope" (Bloch, 1097, 1088). By valorizing music in *Pierre,* Melville gives voice to those excluded from the structures of representation. When these structures begin to crack and crumble, a vision of a more just society can emerge.

8

THE "TINHORN"
REBELLION

ONE WAY TO BRING the previous discussions of enthusiasm and the valorization of music in *Pierre* into a more pointed political context is by focusing on the text's relation to the popular genre of melodrama. Melodrama is the generic home of the enthusiast where the "idea of the good [is] conjoined with [strong] affection" (Kant, *Judgment,* 112). Melodrama is also, as its name suggests, a form that combines music and drama, with the nonrepresentational art form of music functioning in the drama as an indicator of that which lies beyond representation. Melodrama in Melville's day gave voice to those unrepresented in society. In order to understand how Melville's adoption of this form in *Pierre* is related to his desire to "carry republican progressiveness into Literature," we need to examine the historical roots of melodrama and its significance in the early part of the nineteenth century ("Hawthorne and His Mosses," 543).

Although many have commented on the presence of melodrama in *Pierre,* there is no general agreement about the role such elements play in the text.[1] Much of *Pierre*'s peculiarity stems from the jarring presence of melodramatic elements, elements seemingly at odds with the high level of artistry we have come to expect from one of our most gifted writers. The exaggerated and excessively artificial prose style, the contrived and sensational formulaic plot, the stereotypical characters—all are controversial elements in *Pierre* that can be seen to derive from the conventions of contemporary popular melodrama. One cannot help but hear the familiar echoes of melodrama, for example, when Pierre, "smit" by the "most piteous tale" of Ned's seduction of Delly, cries out in righteous indignation: "Curses, wasp-like, cohere on that villain, Ned, and sting him to his death!" (155). Pierre assumes the role of the virtuous hero rescuing the oppressed and victimized women, Delly and Isabel. Lucy is the sheltered innocent, Isabel the dark lady, Ned the reprehensible villain—all easily recognizable stock characters from the melodramatic repertoire. Some see the melodrama in *Pierre* as an "unfortunate lapse" of Melville's talent, in which the author, exhausted and depleted after finishing his great masterpiece, *Moby-Dick*, reached vainly for lofty tragedy in *Pierre*, only to sink miserably into "crude melodrama." [2]

Many critics coming to the defense of Melville think the melodramatic quality of the text represents Melville's satire of the popular form, a rather condescending attempt by the author to pander to the low tastes of the masses while mocking them for not appreciating his art. There is, however, a third possibility that few have considered: that Melville found something of value in the genre of melodrama, that he took the melodramatic form far more seriously than we have imagined. If we keep in mind Melville's portrait of the enthusiast and the valorization of music in *Pierre* along with our insight into the political-ethical implications of Melville's exploration of the limits of representation, we can begin to understand what it was about melodrama that could possibly have interested Melville in the writing of *Pierre*.[3]

First, however, we must move beyond the common pejorative use of the term. Critics of melodrama such as Brooks, Mulvey, and Bentley, and cultural historians Rahill, Grimsted, and Booth have done a great deal to redeem melodrama from many of the negative connotations it holds for twentieth-century readers. Since Melville's day, with the advent of realism and modernism's fascination with moral ambiguity, melodrama has fallen into disfavor, especially among many critics of the classic works of American literature. It is not safe to assume, however, that what we know of Melville's commitment to exploring moral ambiguity in his art necessarily precludes any interest in melodrama. Melville follows the conventions of melodrama as far as they will take him in *Pierre*. Even if in the end he forges his own path among the ambiguities, on the way he gives free rein to the rhetoric and to many of the standard themes of melodrama.

Despite its ultimate ambiguities, *Pierre* is a painstaking study of the nature of good and evil, virtue and vice, set in a typically melodramatic context of social inequality. In contrast to tragedy, which is primarily concerned with exploring human limitations in the face of inexplicable universal forces like nature or God, melodrama focuses on society's injustices as seen from the perspective of the socially oppressed and marginalized. A typically melodramatic plot, for example, involves conflict between the landlords and the landless in which the lecherous landlord tries to seduce the virtuous daughter of the impoverished widow while threatening to foreclose on the mortgage. According to David Grimsted in *Melodrama Unveiled,* class divisions and hostilities were finding expression in the melodramas of Melville's day as good and evil were typically divided along class lines (193). Michael Booth also notes the tendency to represent the upper class as "heartless seducers and oppressors." "Four out of five villains," he writes, will be a "local peer or landowner bent on corrupting the heroine and evicting or imprisoning the father to get to her. [The] profligacy and savagery of the ennobled and propertied class [was] dramatically essential" to melodrama. Virtue was synonymous with "toil, simplicity, poverty," whereas vice denoted "riches, idleness, and property" (123, 62). Frank Rahill concludes that the early, or "classical," melodrama of Melville's day was "proletariat" in spirit (xv).

Pierre shares melodrama's concern with the injustices of the class structure. Most of the melodramatic language in the book is attributed to the enthusiast Pierre, upholding democratic values as he cries out against the real evils of social injustice. *Pierre*'s melodramatic rhetoric does not represent Melville's failed attempt at tragedy. Although the speech in both melodrama and tragedy is similarly "artificial" and highly stylized, Melville clearly distinguishes between the language of tragedy, which we find in Ahab's soliloquies, and the melodramatic language we find in *Pierre.* That the language of melodrama in general seems to parody the language of tragedy is no accident. Melodrama *is* parodying tragedy—in the interests of those traditionally excluded from the center of the tragic stage—the working and servant classes. Melodrama adopts the device of stylized speech to heighten the drama of the lives of the lower classes. With melodrama's focus on social injustice rather than fate, the content and tone of this stylized language changes. The tone of righteous indignation we find in much melodramatic speech stems from the nature of the forces of oppression in melodrama. Something can be done about social injustice; oppressive institutions and hierarchies can be changed, in contrast to the universal forces at work in tragedy. This confrontation with social forces still represents a struggle in melodrama and the happy endings were not a generic necessity in its early forms (Grimsted, 171). It is melodrama's doses of romance and wish fulfillment designed to feed the frustrated desires of the socially and politically powerless that tend to distinguish it from tragedy. The much maligned tears melodrama "jerks" from its audience and the feelings of self-pity it often evokes are what Eric Bentley calls "the poor man's catharsis" and his or her "weapon for survival" (194).[4] Melodrama needs to be understood in this social, economic, and political context of class conflict.

The elitist assumption that Melville pitted himself against popular culture—the assumption behind the claim that he used melodrama to mock the tastes of the masses—has fortunately begun to come into question, notably in the work of David Reynolds. Melville's use of popular genres, like melodrama in *Pierre,* need not be seen as merely a cynical attempt to write a popular book or to parody the base tastes of the public. Melville was not a cultural snob.[5] In general, Melville's treatment of popular forms in his work is free of condescension and indicative of his commitment to egalitarian democracy. Genres represent minisubcultures; they are pockets of significance that the author can use to explore cultural values. Melville's magnanimous treatment of popular forms can be seen in the context of his cultural relativism. Melville made valuable use of such genres as the penny pamphlet in *Israel Potter,* the temperance tale in *Moby-Dick,* and the sailor's ballad in *Billy Budd.* These genres were thriving in Melville's day, and they reflected the interests of many working- and lower-class people. Melville found in the various voices of popular culture a rich resource to be tapped in implementing his artistic-political agenda. The incorporation of popular forms in his work was one method he used to explore the meaning of democracy and to embody in artistic form and content democratic values.

David Reynolds has made an enormous contribution to the study of Melville's relationship to popular culture, but his distinction between "subversive" and "conventional" genres (and subsequent valorization of the former) is a difficult one to maintain. As Jane Tompkins has demonstrated in her reading of nineteenth-century sentimentalism and *Uncle*

Tom's Cabin, even a "conventional" form like melodrama can be shown to contain much of the subversive energy that would have appealed to Melville's egalitarian sentiments. Genres change over the years and become co-opted by various forces in society. Melodrama, a mode that originally had its roots in a democratic and revolutionary working-class culture, was appropriated in the latter part of the nineteenth century by middle-class interests. As it was patronized by the emerging bourgeoisie in America and Europe, it lost a great deal of its democratic associations and took on a more psychological aspect (see Booth, 52; Rahill, xv). Melodrama has undergone so many changes since Melville's day that it is necessary for our purposes to bracket these latter developments and focus on the historical conditions surrounding the emergence of the melodramatic form in the late eighteenth and early nineteenth centuries.[6]

The genre of melodrama has a dual origin. The term *melodrame* appears to have been coined by Rousseau in 1770 to describe his dramatic piece *Pygmalion,* in which he interspersed dialogue with musical interludes intended to suggest an emotional dimension to the drama that could not be captured in words alone. In another part of Paris melodrama was being invented in the popular theaters frequented by the lower classes along the so-called Boulevard du Crime (Brooks, 14). These working-class theaters were forbidden by royal censors and the monopoly of the Theatre-Francais to perform plays with words, so they developed their own elaborate dramatic vocabulary of spectacle, music, and gesture.[7] When use of the spoken word was finally permitted after the revolution, it tended to be highly artificial and play a subordinate role in the drama.

In contrast to tragedy, melodrama has never been much concerned with the "niceties of language" (Rahill, 44). As a reflection of melodrama's indifference to words, it was common to have a crucial turn in the plot depend on a mute or even an animal, such as a dog (see Booth, 86; Grimsted, 102). It is important for our purposes to see in melodrama's origins the mode's characteristic ambivalence toward language and its use of the nonrepresentational art form of music to emphasize the limits of language and representation; these are central themes in *Pierre* that can be related to contemporary melodrama. We also need to keep in mind melodrama's historical context of class conflict, particularly in relation to its linguistic ambivalence and its subsequent valorization of music. When the lower-class theaters, denied the power of words, turned to music in their dramas, the nonrepresentational art form of music functioned as a political tool for representing the interests of the politically unrepresented. Melville uses this tool in *Pierre* through Isabel's music. Melodrama represented the interests of those unrepresented politically, the disenfranchised and illiterate lower classes who dreamed of overthrowing their oppressors.[8] Grimsted has called melodrama "the echo of the historically voiceless" (80). Kirstin Herzog, in *Women, Ethnics, and Exotics,* notes the mode's appeal for women and black writers in the nineteenth century. Because writers like Stowe and Brown were "among the first to articulate the voice of the voiceless, they were not able to leave melodrama behind" (184).

In *Pierre* Melville explores the differences between tragedy and melodrama in terms of class. At times he seems to be mourning the modern loss of the tragic vision, what the narrator calls the loss of the "Hamletism" of the ancient world, which he sees embodied in the Memnon statue: "But Memnon's sculptured woes did once melodiously resound; now all is mute. Fit emblem that of old, poetry was a consecration and an obsequy to all hapless modes of human life, but in a bantering, barren, and prosaic, heartless age, Aurora's music moan is lost among our drifting sands, which whelm alike the monument and the dirge." *Pierre* seems to be Melville's attempt to democratize tragedy. He begins in the tragic mode to establish Pierre's elevated status by tracing his aristocratic lineage. He places Pierre on a "noble pedestal" in preparation for the eventual fall, so that no one will "dream that the last chapter was merely intended for a foolish bravado, and not with a solid purpose in view." Then the narrator addresses those class-conscious readers who might object to Pierre's family pride as showing him to be "no sterling Democrat. . . . I beg you to consider again that this Pierre was but a youngster as yet. And believe me you will pronounce Pierre a thoroughgoing Democrat in time; perhaps a little too Radical altogether to your fancy" (136, 12, 13). In his attempt to democratize tragedy, Melville taps into the reformist, idealist, and democratic roots of melodrama. Melville was evoking the egalitarian democratic spirit of his age when he incorporated the rhetoric and themes of melodrama in *Pierre.* According to Grimsted, melodrama embodied "democratic society's attitude toward morality and nature, its enthusiasm for democracy and domesticity, its tacit separation of the world into spheres of the practical and the transcendent, its desire to see ordinary lives taken seriously and yet be charged with excitement, and its faith in and doubts about progress and providence" (Grimsted, xi).

Melville's use of melodrama in *Pierre* cannot be understood as simply parodic in a negative sense. Melodrama is the generic home of the "enthusiast"; and as Melville treats Pierre's enthusiasm, so he treats the rhetoric of melodrama—ambivalently, but with more than a degree of sympathy. Take, for example, Pierre's melodramatic outburst to Glen and Fred when they try to force Lucy to leave the Church of the Apostles. Pierre cries, "I render no accounts: I am what I am. This sweet girl—this angel whom ye defile by your touches—she is of age by the law—she is her own mistress by the law. And now, I swear she shall have her will! Unhand the girl!" Pierre defends Lucy's freedom to make her own choices and determine the course of her life in an enthusiastic expression of democratic sentiment that would no doubt garner applause from the audience were the scene played out on the stage of a contemporary nineteenth-century theater. In Melville's adoption of this melodramatic stance, I hear a tone of sincerity ringing in sympathy with the democratic sentiments informing Pierre's rhetoric. At the same time, however, the scene evokes ambiguous feelings. Lucy's choice takes her one step closer to death. Understandably, her brother and friend want to prevent her from giving up the comfort and status associated with her family to "join company with the wretched rush-lights of poverty and woe." At the same time, my heart goes out to that doomed little commune as they try to make their way in the wide, wide world, scorning appearance and social conventions (325, 111).

By emphasizing the earnestness of Melville's engagement with melodrama, I do not mean to discount the presence in *Pierre* of Melville the gifted satirist. We need to rethink, however, the critical perception that reduces this satire to disdain for popular sentimental and melodramatic modes. The most bitter satire in *Pierre* appears in the "Young America" chapter and seems to be directed primarily against the genteel members of the literary establishment, the critics and publishers who praised Melville's earlier work (which Melville considered mediocre), but ignored and misunderstood the greatness of *Moby-Dick*. In this chapter and the other clearly satirical opening chapter on the subject of Lucy's and Pierre's love affair, we find the favorite targets of Melville's satirical wit: moral complacency and superficiality. Critics of the poet Pierre's early work, for example, praise the young writer for being "blameless in morals, and harmless throughout," for having as his "predominant end and aim . . . evangelical piety." They are full of admiration for his "Perfect Taste" and the "highly judicious smoothness and genteelness of the sentiments and fancies expressed." One critic concludes about the writer of "The Tropical Summer: A Sonnet," that he is "unquestionably a highly respectable youth" (342–43).

In the chapter entitled "Love, Delight, and Alarm" the narrator praises the beauty of the earth and evinces a belief in moral progress: "From each successive world, the demon Principle is more and more dislodged." He sings in praise of Love, "both Creator's and Saviour's gospel to mankind; a volume bound in rose-leaves, clasped with violets, and by the beaks of humming-birds printed with peach-juice on the leaves of lilies" (44, 45). Melville's ironic distance from the language in these chapters has often been noted; we need to keep in mind, however, that he disdains the superficial moralistic readings of many literary critics because he is deeply concerned with freedom and the relation between ethics and art. Furthermore, he may be mocking the notion of progress, but he professes a belief in the "difference" made by the Declaration of Independence (*Letters*, 80). Melville's satire is primarily directed not against popular forms per se, but against the superficiality and complacency exhibited by those who think they can simply "shut the gate" against "the villains, Want and Woe" and send them with "their sire, the demon Principle . . . back to chaos, whence they came" (44). In contrast, the "ungenteel" genre of melodrama directly confronts such villains and dares to call them by name. Melville may be taking a popular form like melodrama seriously because melodrama takes evil seriously.

In keeping with the class-conscious conventions of melodrama in Melville's day, he presents his villains in *Pierre* as cold, cruel, aristocratic snobs who would turn against the members of their own family to preserve the pure blood of their economic standing. In representing the villainy of the upper class, Melville is tugging at his reader's egalitarian, democratic heartstrings. The most melodramatic scenes in the book involve the conflict between Pierre and his cousin, Glen Stanley. Who can forgive Glen for denying that he knows his own cousin at that glamorous city party and turning Pierre out into the street at night, all because he has married outside their class? The "haughty" Mrs. Glendinning is also presented unsympathetically when she coldly and abruptly cuts Pierre off and leaves the entire estate to that obnoxious Glen. After Pierre's mother dies, when Pierre finally shoots Glen and cries, "For thy one blow, take here two deaths! 'Tis speechless sweet to murder thee!" Pierre, our radical democrat hero, brings to an end his family's dynasty and their long monopolization of the land (502).

In *Pierre* we find Melville close to openly declaring his radical democrat allegiance in the long digression on pedigrees where he takes up the cause of the Anti-Renters, the farmer-tenants around Albany who rebelled in 1839 against the semi-feudalism of the old Dutch patroon estates in upstate New York. Melville's support of the farmer-tenants was indeed radical for its time. Cooper expressed his support of the landlords in several novels, and even Whitman opposed the Anti-Rent agitators. In sympathizing with the farmer tenants, Melville courageously pits himself not only against these and other prominent Americans, but against his own family, for his mother, Maria Gansevoort, was a proud descendent of the first patroon, Kiliaen Van Rensselaer. The link between democratic sentiment and the genre of melodrama that Melville seems to be exploiting in *Pierre* is evident when we consider the conditions surrounding the popular success in America of the English melodrama *The Rent Day* (1832) by Douglas Jerrold. Jerrold's play became famous in Melville's day, rallying sentiment in upstate New York in support of the Anti-Renters' "tin-horn rebellion" against the Dutch patroons (Rahill, xvii). *The Rent Day* presents the story of a family of tenant farmers threatened with eviction because they cannot make their annual rent payment to an absentee landlord. It was one of the first plays to make use of that now stereotypical melodramatic device—the foreclosed mortgage. Melville could have seen this play as it was performed throughout the 1830s and 1840s in New York City and in riverboats along the Hudson river (Rahill, 162). Melville, in declaring *Pierre* to be "calculated for popularity" may have been trying to tap the same anti-landlord sentiment that fueled the success in New York State of Jerrold's popular melodrama (*Letters,* 150).[9]

At least one contemporary reader of *Pierre* recognized the importance of this now rather obscure political context surrounding the novel when he wrote in his review of the book that it has "something to do with the Patroons and the anti-renters."[10] The patroonships were an anachronism in nineteenth-century America, a carryover from prerevolutionary times. In 1629 Kiliaen Van Rensselaer, a pearl and diamond merchant in Amsterdam, along with several other Dutch businessmen, obtained a charter from the Dutch West India Company to establish colonies in the New World. Their "true purpose," however, was to "wage privateer war against Spanish ships carrying gold and silver from Peru and Mexico." Enormous wealth was accumulated by the company through this venture and eventually land was granted along the Hudson river to any member who would plant a colony. To encourage colonization, the Company offered members absolute power as patroon consisting of "baronial authority, with full property rights and complete civil and military control over the people, who would be bound by contract to fealty and military service as vassals" (Christman, 2, 3). The patroon system survived through the revolutionary war and well into the nineteenth century. The leases of the farmer-tenants were "durable," that is, to be held in perpetuity with a yearly rent to be paid in money, crops, or service on Rent Day, the first Tuesday of January (Miller, 64). A few families descending from the patroons, through an intricate system of intermarriage, came to control three hundred thousand people and 2 million acres, monopolizing almost all the land within a 150-mile radius of Albany, where Melville lived as a boy (Christman, 1).

In 1839 the last official patroon, Stephen Van Rensselaer III, died. His estate, Rensselaerwyck, "embraced all of Albany and Rensselaer counties and part of Columbia, and by 1838 was maintaining between sixty and one hundred thousand tenant farmers." Van Rensselaer doubted the legality of his leases and had hesitated to collect back rents for years. For this he was called the "good patroon." When he died, however, he left a will that stipulated that his debts be paid out of the four hundred thousand dollars owed in rents so as not to diminish his sons' inheritance. The tenant farmers protested, claiming that they had a moral right to the land, that they had paid its purchase price and taxes many times over. The heir, Stephen Van Rensselaer IV, refused to negotiate.

On 4 July 1839, the Anti-Renters assembled at Berne, the highest point in the Helderberg hills, to make their "Declaration of Independence" (Christman, 2, 20).

When the land agents and sheriffs came to collect the rents, the warning sounds of the farmers' tin dinner horns echoed through the hills. The tenants, dressed as Indians in calico, tarred and feathered many an emissary of the Van Rensselaers. In December 1839 Governor Seward called up the state militia to wage war on the rebellious Anti-Renters. Seven hundred troops marched into the hills. No blood was shed this time—and no rents collected—but armed struggles persisted and increased in violence for a period of thirty more years. In 1846 the Anti-Renters exerted enough political pressure to call for a State Constitutional Convention. For the first time in the history of the state, the convention was not dominated by upper- and middle-class interests: fifty-three of the delegates were farmers and mechanics. The Anti-Renters demanded "equal rights without regard to race, and asserted that there should be no qualifications for any right, trust, or profession except merit, integrity, and ability." Eventually, many Anti-Renters were to join forces with the National reformers and the abolitionists to form the Free Soil party. In 1850 the Supreme Court finally found Van Rensselaer's titles invalid. Van Rensselaer sold out, but the new landlord, through appeals and technicalities, continued to collect rents from the farmers for many years to come (Christman, 258, 264, 291).[11]

Because social status in America was based on wealth, with relatively few clear-cut class distinctions, the American aristocracy was extremely exclusive. In order to preserve social difference, it discriminated harshly against the lower classes. Many aristocratic families went to great lengths to establish impressive genealogies (Miller, 78–79). In *Pierre* Melville refers to the Anti-Rent agitation within the context of the narrator's attempt to establish the "great genealogical and real-estate dignity" of Pierre's aristocratic family heritage. For Pierre, his land rights seemed "sanctified through their very long uninterrupted possession by his race" (8). Henry Murray, commenting on the "digressive remarks" in *Pierre* on the "topic of estates and pedigrees" (remarks that include Melville's discussion of the Tinhorn Rebellion), concludes that they represent Melville "the Anglophile" speaking in "defense of the disappearing American 'aristocracy'" (435–36). On the contrary, Melville is not defending the aristocracy. His remarks are a response to those who claim that America has no class structure—regardless of whether they see this alleged "classlessness" as a sign of progress or barbarity. Melville tries to set the record straight in *Pierre*.

America may have no "chartered aristocracy, and no law of entail," but it still has a class structure. Although it is true that the "democratic element" acts as nature does "forever producing new things by corroding the old," it is also true that there are "things in the visible world, over which ever-shifting Nature hath not so unbounded a sway." Some families, for example, are like blades of grass "annually changed"; some are like oak trees "putting forth new branches; whereby Time, instead of subtracting, is made to capitulate into a multiple virtue." This may seem at first to be Melville's "natural" justification of social hierarchy; but his use of the word *capitulate* harks back to a previous passage in which Pierre—the only male with the Glendinning surname—dreams of having a "monopoly of glory in capping the fame-column, whose tall shaft had been erected by his noble sires." The fiduciary imagery in these passages suggests that "capital" is that thing "over which ever-shifting Nature hath not so unbounded a sway." But in spite of man's proud efforts to glorify himself through capital, the narrator predicts that "Nature" will have the final word. The quarries and ruins of Palmyra teach a "foreboding and prophetic lesson. . . . Among those ruins is a crumbling, uncompleted shaft, and some leagues off, ages ago left in the quarry, is the crumbling corresponding capital, also incomplete. These Time seized and spoiled; these Time crushed in the egg; and the proud stone that should have stood among the clouds, Time left abased beneath the soil" (10, 9, 7–8). And so it goes also with the seemingly timeless Dutch Manors of New York's Hudson Valley. The patroon's

> haughty rent-deeds are held by their thousand farmer tenants, so long as grass grows and water runs; which hints of a surprising eternity for a deed, and seems to make lawyer's ink unobliterable as the sea. . . .
>
> These far-descended Dutch meadows lie steeped in a Hindooish haze; an eastern patriarchalness sways its mild crook over pastures, whose tenant flocks shall there feed, long as their own grass grows, long as their own water shall run. Such estates seem to defy Time's

tooth, and by conditions which take hold of the indestructible earth seem to cotemporize their fee-simples with eternity. Unimaginable audacity of a worm that but crawls through the soil he so imperially claims! (*Pierre,* 11)

In contrast to the English lords who point to the past and boast of their ancestors retaining "three-hundred men-at-arms," our American "lords . . . point to the present." As evidence, the narrator evokes the historical moment when Van Rensselaer enlisted the force of the state militia to crush the tinhorn rebellion:

> One will show you that the public census of a county, is but part of the roll of his tenants. Ranges of mountains, high as Ben Nevis or Snowdon, are their walls; and regular armies, with staffs of officers, crossing rivers with artillery, and marching through primeval woods, and threading vast rocky defiles, have been sent out to distrain upon three thousand farmer-tenants of one landlord, at a blow. A fact most suggestive two ways; both whereof shall be nameless here. (11)

This "fact" is suggestive of the discrepancy between democratic ideals and political expediencies and the complicity between governmental forces and the private financial interests of the upper class. *Pierre*'s narrator concludes his remarks by condescending to those like Cooper who try to bolster America's reputation in Europe by praising her aristocratic class: should America "choose to glorify herself in that inconsiderable way . . . [she will] make out a good general case with England in this short little matter of large estates, and long pedigrees." Melville's treatment of the American class structure is not, in contrast to Cooper's, intended to glorify America; rather it is to "poetically establish the richly aristocratic condition" of Pierre as necessary for an understanding of subsequent developments. In order to understand this book, in other words, you need to understand class in America (11, 13).

In typically melodramatic fashion Melville targets the mortgage, the "haughty rent-deed," that "nominal title" by which such "mighty lordships" have survived the "Revolutionary flood" in the "heart of a republic," that piece of paper that seems "to make lawyer's ink unobliterable as the sea." Symptomatic of melodrama's ambivalence toward language, this focus in *Pierre* on the proud deed is linked in turn to the book's thematics of the proper name, especially as names are used to buttress hereditary hierarchical class structures. Pierre's pride in his family name and his dream of monopoly, it is suggested, make him ripe for his eventual fall.[12] The narrator warns that "the magnificence of names must not mislead us as to the humility of things." As an example of the "ill-match" between name and thing, he points to the bastards in the English Peerage. "All honour to the names then, and all courtesy to the men; but if St. Albans tell me he is all-honourable and all-eternal, I must still politely refer him to Nell Gwynne" (II, 9, 10).

Melville draws on melodrama's ambivalence to language and valorization of music to bring the reader face to face with the limits to representation. These limits, however, prevent Melville from totally embracing the manichean universe of melodrama. Pierre, the enthusiast, victim of "Civilization, Philosophy, and Ideal Virtue," is also the victim of the melodramatic imagination itself, as Pierre himself eventually comes to realize. When Isabel asks Pierre, near the end of their journey together, to teach her the meanings of the words vice and virtue, those semantic distinctions upon which melodrama depends fade into nothingness. "Look," says Pierre, "a nothing is the substance, it cast one shadow one way, and another the other way; and these two shadows cast from one nothing; these, seems to me, are Virtue and Vice." Isabel wants to know why, then, does he torment himself so. Because, Pierre replies, "It is the law . . . that a nothing should torment a nothing" (302, 274).

Melodrama's power for the people of Melville's day derived "from the tension it suggested between a threatening common reality and the perfect structure it upheld as a morally necessary transcendent reality" (Grimsted, 324). It is this ambivalent tension that fuels *Pierre,* the tension between the horological and chronometrical that is the subject of Plinlimmon's pamphlet. The world *should* have an "ear for Earnestness," Melville seems to be pleading (264). A transcendent reality *is* a moral necessity. But in order to be truly transcendent, this reality must be, as Kant argues, beyond representation in any positive sense. And so, whereas melodrama has served many of Melville's needs in *Pierre,* even up until the book's final melodramatic tableau, the representation of moral ambiguity becomes in *Pierre,* as in all Melville's works, an ethical-aesthetic imperative.

CONCLUSION

9

ALONG SUBLIME FRONTIERS: A WOMAN'S STORY

IN *PIERRE* MELVILLE'S JOURNEY to the sublime limits of representation brings him to the world of women. The encounter with Isabel appears to set off a chain reaction in Melville's work as he returns again and again in the short fiction written immediately after *Pierre* to diptych structures and representations of marginalized women. Stories such as "The Paradise of Bachelors and the Tartarus of Maids," "The Piazza," "The Bell Tower," and "The Encantadas" have all been shown to contain critiques of society's exclusion and oppression of women, particularly women of the underclasses.[1] This concluding chapter will select from the short fiction as it reflects on the preceding argument about the politics of Melville's aesthetic. Following a trajectory originating in the gendered juxtaposition of the diptych *Moby-Dick* and *Pierre,* I trace a course through the stories touching on our central configuration of class, gender, sublime aesthetics, and egalitarian ethics. "The Piazza" represents our telos, the perfect vantage point from which to view the various thematic strands introduced above.[2] It provides us with a conclusion circumscribed by Melville himself, a retrospective view of the development of his own aesthetic journey in the form of a sublime quest that meets its limits in a woman's story. This conclusion brings me full circle as I reflect on my own experience as a woman reading Melville's texts.

Conclusion

Pierre is the first Melville text I ever read, and I was astounded to find in it a woman, Isabel, with whom I could identify. Melville's treatment of class injustices particularly impressed me. I consider his texts valuable allies in the quest to democratize literary and cultural studies. Apparently, my introduction to Melville through *Pierre* has contributed to skewing my perception of his work away from the critical norm. Feminist colleagues, especially, have asked me, "Why do you want to work on the enemy?" I find in Melville's texts uncommon sensitivity to the injustices around issues of class, gender, sexuality, ethnicity. Perhaps his contribution is often misunderstood and overlooked because of our primary critical focus on *Moby-Dick*.[3] I am not suggesting that we supplant *Moby-Dick*, just that we keep in mind the polar structure of Melville's thought, in general, and his fondness for diptychs. As panoramic in scope as *Moby-Dick* is, it is not the total picture.

Moby-Dick has represented, for feminists and traditional critics alike, a bastion of masculinist ideology where women are as out of place as Aunt Charity's ginger beer on the *Pequod*. Often used to buttress theories of American literature that valorize male bonding and the romantic quest into the wilderness away from home and mother, *Moby-Dick* is an exemplary text for its generic representation from a male perspective of the segregation of the sexes in nineteenth-century America.[4] Melville himself apparently thought of *Moby-Dick* as a man's book and wrote to one of his female friends, Sarah Moorehead, to dissuade her from reading it for fear of offending her feminine sensibilities: "Dont you buy it—dont even read it, when it does come out, because it is by no means the sort of book for you. It is not a piece of fine, feminine, Spitalfield silk—but is of the horrible texture of a fabric that should be woven of ship's cables and hausers." When Sophia Hawthorne wrote to Melville praising the book, his response was one of astonishment: "I have hunted up the finest Bath I could find, gilt-edged and stamped, whereon to inscribe my humble acknowledgement of your highly flattering letter of the 29th of Dec:—It really amazed me that you should find any satisfaction in that book. It is true that some *men* have said they were pleased with it but you are the only *woman*—for as a general thing, women have small taste for the sea. . . . Next time [I shall not send you a] bowl of salt water. . . . The next chalice I shall commend, will be a rural bowl of milk." He then inquires politely about the state of her "domestic affairs" (*Letters*, 138, 145–46).

Melville's remarks to both these women suggest that he was working at this time under certain gender-determined notions of genre. If genres represent minisubcultures with their own values, languages, epistemologies, and so on, then it seems understandable that in a period characterized by relatively separate spheres for men and women, there would be associated with each sphere types of literary works that best reflect that group's immediate concerns.[5] Melville had been working most of his career with a predominantly male audience in mind. In the six novels leading up to and including *Moby-Dick*—sea adventures all—women appear as either obstacles to the male romantic quest or as the distant and unattainable object of that quest. *Pierre,* which Melville referred to generically as a "regular romance," marks a definite shift away from the man's world of the sea adventure to the land-locked domestic world of women. In *Pierre* we find Melville finally giving his female characters articulation and beginning to face, on a generic level, the challenge that the female community presented to male writers like himself who had excluded them for too long. If women barely make it to the margins of *Moby-Dick,* the woman as artist takes center stage in *Pierre.*[6]

For many readers *Pierre* represents Melville's Waterloo. One cannot help but wonder what could have led Melville, at the height of his creative powers, to plunge into the alien territory of the domestic romance. After pursuing the romantic quest into the wilderness to its limits in *Moby-Dick,* Melville turns to its generic "opposite," the domestic romance, and takes that to its limits also. The familiar trope of the "ship as world," which had served Melville well for years, tended to exclude the female half of the population. *Pierre*'s setting provides Melville with the opportunity to explore the world of women excluded from his earlier works and to address a nineteenth-century female audience largely concerned with domesticity, Christianity, and the position of women in society. Through his use of the diptych structure, Melville represents the totality of his world while at the same time inscribing gender exclusivity.

In several short stories written immediately after *Pierre,* "Two Temples," "Poor Man's Pudding and Rich Man's Crumbs," and "The Paradise of Bachelors and the Tartarus of Maids," Melville uses the diptych structure to mark polarization and exclusion based on gender and class. Each diptych juxtaposes two separately set tales told by the same first-person narrator. "The Paradise of Bachelors and the Tartarus of

Maids" offers the clearest reflection on the gender-determined relation between *Moby-Dick* and *Pierre*. This story has been read as a celebration of the homoerotic joys of bachelorhood and an example of Melville's alleged misogyny. But as the more careful readers of Melville's alleged "racist" texts have demonstrated, Melville likes to set ideological traps to catch readers in their own prejudices. The methods used by Carolyn L. Karcher, for example, in her readings of Melville's texts dealing with racial oppression need to be applied to his texts about sexual oppression as well (Karcher, xii). As Jane Mushabac writes, "Melville had always been profoundly attuned to the condition of slavery implicit in the human condition; it was only a matter of time before he noticed that women as well as men were slaves" (149). In *Pierre* the figure of Isabel has opened Melville's eyes to the condition of women who live on the margins of society—impoverished, excluded, abused, and exploited women, like the workers in "The Tartarus of Maids." The gendered juxtaposition of the diptych "The Paradise of Bachelors and the Tartarus of Maids" illustrates not only women's exclusion but also their constitutive status in capitalistic, patriarchal society. Setting the story in a paper factory serves to emphasize representation's complicity in women's exploitation. The "blank looking girls, with blank, white folders in their blank hands, all blankly folding blank paper" must surrender their reproductive power (the factory will only employ "maids") in the production of paper that the wealthy bachelor lawyers in the first tale will inscribe with the language of money (328). The diptych structure here implies that the extravagant lifestyle of the lawyer bachelors is linked—even depends upon—the deprivation of the oppressed maids at work in the paper factory.

Melville certainly deserves more credit than he has gotten for addressing the concerns of women.[7] He is often judged guilty by his association with Hawthorne whose notorious remarks about "that damned mob of scribbling women" seem to have attached themselves to Melville as well. Jane Tompkins, for example, claims that Melville along with Hawthorne "hated" the popular and critical success of "their sentimental rivals" (148). In contrast to Hawthorne, who fled to Europe expressing disgust with the women writers he believed were edging him out of a writer's living, Melville weathered the storm and even appears to have made a bid for position in the changing market with *Pierre*. Surprisingly, Hawthorne's derogatory remarks about women writers have done little to damage his reputation among male and female readers today who admire his strong female characters. Melville, on the other hand, has been attacked by feminist critics, because of his "inability" to move beyond stereotypes to present realistic, fully developed, strong, and positive female characters.[8]

In the "Agatha" letters written to Hawthorne after Melville completed *Pierre*, Melville appears to be experiencing a crisis of confidence concerning his ability to represent women. He seems painfully aware of this literary "shortcoming" in comparison to Hawthorne, whom he urges to write a story based on information Melville had collected about a woman named Agatha. This woman witnesses the shipwreck of her husband and nurses him back to health only to see him off again. She spends the rest of her life waiting in vain for his return; he marries and raises a family in another port (*Letters*, 154–61). It seems for the first time that Melville's imagination and sympathy are engaged more with the woman left on shore than the sailor at sea. He pesters Hawthorne to write the woman's story because, he says, it is in Hawthorne's "vein." Hawthorne finally loses patience with his friend, and tells him to write it himself. The Agatha letters were written during the time when Hawthorne was trying to distance himself from Melville. Perhaps Melville's sympathy for the Agatha figure is linked to his own feelings of being abandoned by the one whom he tries to force to write her story. We do not know whether Melville ever did write Agatha's story.[9] Agatha's story seems to have inspired Melville's story of Hunilla in "The Encantadas," the Chola woman who witnesses from the shore the drowning of her husband and brother and is left alone on a remote, wilderness island. Out of respect for Hunilla, the narrator marks the limits to his powers of representation when he vaguely hints that she is the victim of an unspeakable crime by the hands of a passing whale ship. In tribute to Hunilla's character, Melville writes, "Humanity, thou strong thing, I worship thee, not in the laurelled victor, but in this vanquished one" (157).

Perhaps Melville's interest in women's lives has often been overlooked because he does not tend to represent strong, middle-class women triumphing over adversity in a man's world, the kind of woman we find in Fanny Fern's *Ruth Hall*—a book that won Hawthorne's praise.[10] The strong women in Melville's work, like Hautia in *Mardi* and Mrs. Glendinning in *Pierre,* are oppressors, like Melville's strong man, Ahab. Such strength as theirs is more like abuse of power. Through these women, Melville explores the darker side of women's political powerlessness, which leads in the case of Pierre's mother, for example, to excessive control over the domestic realm. Mrs. Glendinning rules supreme over her maternal domain with the church, in the figure of the ineffectual Reverend Falsgrave, at her side—illustrating the nineteenth century's strategic alliance that Ann Douglas has documented and critiqued in *The Feminization of American Culture.* Melville's representation of the darker side of family life in *Pierre* has led one historian to praise him as his period's "most insightful critic of ante-bellum domesticity" (Ryan, 126). Although Ryan gives Melville credit for his insightful cultural critique, she and other less generous critics place undue emphasis on *Pierre's* negativity, emphasis that has led to the conclusion that Melville hated sentimentalism.[11]

On the contrary, Melville's own declaration of allegiance to "the heart" in a letter to Hawthorne aligns him with much of *Pierre's* enthusiastic and sentimental rhetoric (*Letters,* 129; see chap. 6). *Pierre* is a book about righteousness and the transforming power of love, in sentiment and passion comparable to *Uncle Tom's Cabin.*[12] Unlike Stowe, however, Melville has deeply ambivalent feelings about Christianity, which he explores in *Pierre.* On the one hand, he is attracted to that embodiment of all love, the Sermon on the Mount; on the other hand, he despairs at the abyss separating the ideal and the practical in this "mammonish" world. It is a distortion to reduce this ambivalence to purely negative parody, just as it is a mistake to reduce *Pierre* to a cynical and mean-spirited attack on the sentimentalism of the female reading public. Melville was not above eliciting a sentimental response from his reader. In the heartbreaking story of Hunilla's suffering, for example, the narrator warns the reader that "if he feel not, he reads in vain" (156).

Melville seems primarily interested in representing women who may very well be strong, but who, unlike the Ruth Halls and Fanny Ferns of this world, remain oppressed and excluded by social forces. His texts about women need to be seen in relation to the popular generic tradition that David S. Reynolds has identified as "the literature of women's wrongs," including, for example, the works of Rebecca Harding Davis (351–52). Like Isabel's tale in *Pierre,* and like the story of the factory workers in "The Tartarus of Maids," this "literature of women's wrongs" focuses on the struggles of the impoverished and unrepresented working-class women, factory workers and seamstresses. The problem for Melville as a writer is how to represent the unrepresentability of these women—their marginal, yet constitutive, status in a capitalistic, patriarchal world. Excluded from *Moby-Dick* and "The Paradise of Bachelors," these women are elevated by the author to a position of "equality" as the focus of the diptych's second half, *Pierre* and "The Tartarus of Maids," respectively. Through the figure of Isabel, Melville begins to explore the depth of the excluded feminine's subversive power. *Pierre* may be named for a male character, but the moving force in the book is Isabel. Her initial shriek initiates a chain of events that ultimately pulls all around her to destruction. Her power is not merely destructive, however. It is Isabel who awakens Pierre to the "darker though truer aspect of things" (94). For this alone, she deserves to be ranked among Melville's heroes.

Melville's interest in representing women's unrepresentedness may have been sparked by the works of women writers that he was apparently reading at this time: Mary Shelley's *Frankenstein* and Germaine de Staël's *Corinne*.[13] The striking parallels between Victor Frankenstein and Ahab strongly suggest that Melville drew heavily on Shelley's portrait of the monomaniacal Victor in creating his Ahab. In his next writing project, *Pierre,* Melville may have adopted a strategy Shelley uses in *Frankenstein* of interrupting the flow of the narrative with a detailed story told in first person by one oppressed and excluded from the previously dominant discourse. In *Pierre* Isabel's counternarrative telling the story of her life—her extreme loneliness, her awakening sense of self, her struggle to learn to read and write, her search for links with others—reads like the creature's narrative in *Frankenstein*. Both tell of an existence on the margins of representation. Isabel is the sympathetic monster as woman. When Melville decided to present Isabel as a powerful artist—a musician and singer—he may also have had in mind Madame de Staël's influential book *Corinne* (see chapter 6).

Melville's apparent attempts in *Pierre* to reach out to the female reading public of his time were a dismal failure. Perhaps the book's scathing critique of the American class structure told from the point of view of those exploited and excluded, the impoverished servant class, combined with the theme of incest, simply cut the book off from the appreciation of the more genteel, middle-class audience. The highly wrought and densely allusive language may have cut it off as well from the under-educated lower classes. Furthermore, Melville uses an exceedingly artificial language in *Pierre* at a time when the dominant aesthetic in America was beginning to shift toward realism, a generic shift spearheaded by the women writers associated with the local color movement, such as Caroline Kirkland, Alice Carey, and Rose Terry Cooke (Fetterly, 10).

In three short stories written after *Pierre,* "The Bell Tower," "I and My Chimney," and "The Piazza," we find Melville exploring gender-genre conflicts in the context of his quest for the sublime. In "The Bell Tower" the key figure's name, Bannadonna, suggests the exclusive and masculinist quality of an egoistic aesthetic of domination. Related to Ahab, Bannadonna is the fanatic as artist. He acknowledges no limits. "Naught's an obstacle" to Bannadonna's stated purpose to build the highest, grandest tower from which to command a view of the land. When, in the process, he murders a timid worker, the "charitable" impute his act to "esthetic passion, not to any flagitious quality." Bannadonna's aesthetic is quite divorced from the realm of ethics. Others' lives are merely a means to Bannadonna's artistic ends. By setting the story in the Italian renaissance—the culture that invented one-point perspective in the visual arts—Melville exposes the historical roots of egoistic individualist ideology and the sexist domination of nature and others. The architect's death at the hands of his "iron slave" in the tower's clock machinery warns of how "seeking to conquer a larger liberty, man but extends the empire of necessity" (176,174). Melville's critique of Bannadonna's aesthetic is analogous to his critique of Ahab's ethics in *Moby-Dick.* The quest for totality does not necessarily entail the monomaniacal indifference to others. Melville's aesthetic is to be distinguished from Bannadonna's, an aesthetic that is often characterized as the "egoistical" sublime, a term I generally eschew for strategic purpose.[14]

The chimney in "I and My Chimney" functions, like the bell tower, as a phallic and an aesthetic metaphor. Melville's relation to the chimney, however, is more ambiguous and personal, as suggested by the autobiographical references in the text. The narrator's fight to save the chimney from destruction figures Melville's own commitment to sublime aesthetics and the structure of the romantic quest, as it is exemplified in both *Moby-Dick* and *Pierre.* The narrator's beloved old chimney—which he compares to the pyramids and to a whale, two of Melville's favorite images of the sublime—is under attack from several fronts. On the one hand, "mysterious intimations" from one signed "Claude" (representing an aesthetic of the "beautiful" in landscape painting) have appeared in the village newspaper suggesting that "a certain structure, standing on a certain hill, is a sad blemish to an otherwise lovely landscape." On the home front, the narrator's wife and daughters object to the chimney's centralized position in the house, from which it dominates like an autocratic ruler. They wish to tear down the (phallic) chimney to clear the way for a (yonic) "grand entrance-hall" (376, 360).

The argument between the narrator and the women of his house echoes the debates surfacing in the press over the relevance of a romance aesthetic. As Josephine Donovan and Judith Fetterly have demonstrated, women writers of the local color movement, such as Caroline Kirkland, Alice Carey, and Rose Terry Cooke, tapped a "centuries old tradition of women's literary realism opposed to sentimental romance," a tradition rooted in philosophical empiricism and novelistic critiques of romance aesthetics (Donovan, 3). They championed realism as an antidote to the excesses of the romance (Fetterly, 10–11). Solidly middle class and pragmatic, their writing is characterized by a no-nonsense attitude toward reality, emphasis on ordinary people in ordinary settings, simplified language, regionalisms, and a skeptical attitude toward "romanticizing"—particularly as it tended to "idealize" and thereby erase the individuality and subjectivity of women. In comparison to the unpretentious work of these popular local color realists, Melville's writing, with its obscure metaphysics, dense literary allusions, and elaborately figurative language, must have seemed as old-fashioned as the narrator's smoky old chimney.

Whereas "I and My Chimney" leaves the narrator holding fast, not about to succumb to pressure and abandon his commitment to an aesthetics of the sublime, "The Piazza" reflects on the value, limits, and ethical implications of Melville's aesthetic quest for the sublime. This story, the title piece to Melville's only published collection of short fiction, reads as a retrospective of Melville's writing career up to this point. Drawing on the popular genre of the landscape sketch, Melville lays out for his reader a literary map of aesthetic ground covered in his artistic journey. The unnamed first-person narrator, using metaphors that recall the formative influence of Melville's sailing days, tells of an "inland voyage to fairy-land. A true voyage; but take it all in all, interesting as if invented" (4). He launches his yawl to find the source of a light on the mountaintop. The quest culminates in the narrator's encounter with a woman who resembles Isabel. Both Marianna and Isabel are impoverished orphans living with their "brothers" in an abandoned shelter on the margins of human society.

"The Piazza" begins with the narrator's homage to nature as it is found in the landscape surrounding his farmhouse. He needs a piazza from which to contemplate the sights, but he must choose between four prospects. After much deliberation, he rejects the beautiful views of pastures, apple orchards, and rolling hills and decides to build his piazza on the north side facing the sublime Mount Greylock. While gazing at the mountain one day, he spots a shining light and thinks to himself, "Fairies there." (Who, but fairies, would dare to live in such a wild setting?) After an undisclosed illness confines him to his bed, the narrator grows so sensitive that he finds himself disgusted by the cultivated beauty immediately surrounding his home in the valley. He looks closely at the flowers creeping up the post beside his piazza and sees "millions of strange, cankerous worms, which, feeding upon those blossoms, so shared their blessed hue, as to make it unblessed evermore— worms, whose germs had doubtless lurked in the very bulb which, so hopefully, I had planted." To cure himself, the narrator decides to set off for fairyland in search of the source of light shining from the mountaintop (5, 6). Nourished by his readings in the romance tradition, the works of Spenser and Shakespeare, he dreams of finding his fairy queen there, or at least some glad mountain girl, to ease his weariness.

As Richard S. Moore, Helmbrecht Breinig, and Klaus Poenicke have convincingly demonstrated, "The Piazza" represents a journey through the beautiful, the picturesque, and the sublime of nineteenth-century aesthetics. The autobiographical elements in the story invite comparison of the narrator with Melville himself. When the narrator has to choose among four prospects for the placement of his piazza, he decides to direct his gaze to the sublime. He is eventually so repulsed by the mask of beauty that he decides to leave it behind and scale the sublime heights.[15] He begins his quest for the sublime in hopes of finding his fairy queen, Una—the one truth. He travels along the picturesque

mountainside and finds reminders of humanity's failed attempts to conquer nature: an "old saw-mill, bound down and hushed with vines,"
a huge block that someone had tried to split, but that still contains
the "wedges yet rusted in their holes," and, finally, apples from a long-
neglected tree that now taste of the ground (7).

When he reaches the sublime summit, repetition suggests an infinity
beyond representation: "No fence was seen, no inclosure. Near by—
ferns, ferns, ferns; further—woods, woods, woods; beyond—mountains, mountains, mountains; then—sky, sky, sky. Turned out in aerial
commons, pasture for the mountain moon. Nature, and but nature,
house and all." Nature erases culture, the boundary dissolves. The house
on the mountain's summit is dilapidated, its north side is "doorless and
windowless" (in contrast to the narrator's northside piazza). Instead of
meeting his "Una," "Titania," or at least "some glad, mountain girl,"
the narrator finds Marianna, an orphaned young woman who, along
with her brother, has taken up residence on the mountain in an abandoned cottage. Here she works sewing by the only paned window, while
her brother cuts wood and burns coal on the other side of the mountain most of the day and night. When the narrator speaks of Marianna's
house as "gilded"—as it appears to him from his piazza below—she
sharply contradicts him and paints him a bleak picture in realistic detail
of her daily struggle for existence. She tells him of the sun that shines
through the window nearly blinding her at her work, of the flies and
the wasps, the rotting roof, and the chimney that fills with snow in the
winter. When he responds inappropriately, "Yours are strange fancies,
Marianna," she counters: "They but reflect the things," a response that
leaves the narrator "mute" (8, 5, 10). Apparently the "sublimity" of her
natural setting interests her not. When the narrator suggests that she
walk outside to break up the monotony, she explains that being alone
by the hearth is better than being alone by a rock. She is interested in
the beautiful house in the valley, the narrator's house, which she can
see from her window. Inside her own house she finds her comfort and
company in her familiar world of shadows, shadows she has named.

Several critics see Marianna's shadow reading as evidence of her in-
sanity and emphasize the narrator's apparent disappointment at dis-
covering that his hoped-for "fairy queen" is nothing but a poor, mad
woman, defeated rather than uplifted by her sublime surroundings. In

the representation and interpretation of Marianna lies Melville's ideological trap. Seeing Marianna as "possibly demented" or "nearly crushed and extinguished in her humanity" reveals our own gender and class prejudices (Moore, 3; Poenicke, 267). "No doubt you think," says Marianna, "that, living so lonesome here, knowing nothing, hearing nothing—little, at least, but sound of thunder and the fall of trees—never reading, seldom speaking, yet ever wakeful, this is what gives me my strange thoughts—for so you call them—this weariness and wakefulness together." The reader knows, however, (and perhaps Marianna senses), that the narrator, who knows a lot and reads a lot and who calls her thoughts "strange," experiences the same symptoms of weariness and wakefulness, symptoms that drove him to her in the first place to seek the cure. Furthermore, the narrator also reads shadows, the shadow battles on the mountainside, visible from his piazza, the "old wars of Lucifer and Michael" (11, 5). With this identity between the two characters established, their different perspectives seem determined by social, economic, and biological factors.

Rather than interpret Marianna as a "victim" of her sublime environment who reveals the "lie" of sublime aesthetics (Poenicke, 273), perhaps we need to consider her a victim of a socioeconomic system that has forced her, much like Frankenstein's monster among the caves of ice, to seek the only dwelling "man does not grudge" (Shelley, 96). The negative determining factors in Marianna's life seem overwhelming when we consider her poverty, her lack of education, her harsh environment, her isolation, her gender, her work, and so on. Yet to completely reduce her to the status of a "victim" is to deny her autonomy and power of self-determination. If we see her only as "insane," we negate her dignity as a human being. Surely there is something to admire in this young woman who strives to make a life for herself along with her brother under such adverse circumstances. Marianna renders the narrator "mute" on two occasions (9, 10). For Melville, who wrote that "Silence" is the "only Voice of our God," this power of Marianna's deserves respect (*Pierre*, 208). It marks the limits to the narrator's powers of representation.

Rosemary Kenny comes closest to granting Marianna the dignity she deserves. Drawing on the textual allusions to Plato's allegory of the cave, Kenny recognizes in the poor woman an artist. She concludes that through the figure of Marianna Melville is parodying the lesser, "mimetic" artist who, in the Platonic sense, takes shadows for the real things (326). Kenny's characterization of Marianna as a realist artist is useful, particularly when considered in the context of the gender-genre conflicts at this time between realist and romance aesthetics. But Melville allows this character a dignity beyond parody. It is not the realist artist that is the target of Melville's critique in his curious twist on Plato's allegory of the cave, but the hierarchical dimension of Platonic thought itself with its inherent devalorization of matter and the sensory world. The narrator in "The Piazza" scales the heights in search of "Una" the one eternal truth, and finds at the top of the mountain, not Plato's shining light of one truth, but, ironically, in an inversion of Plato's allegory, a cavelike dwelling in which sits a woman, chained to her work, blinded by the sun, reading shadows on the wall. When Marianna says to the narrator, whom she sees looking out the window at the ground, "You watch the cloud," he "corrects" her (as she had earlier "corrected" him about the "gilding" of her house): "No, a shadow; a cloud's, no doubt— though I cannot see," he says, making the "proper" Platonic hierarchical distinctions between appearance and reality, shadow and thing, distinctions that she is either unable—or unwilling—to make (20).

Melville's critique of Platonic idealism here is similar to the critique by Kant we saw earlier. Like the dove who imagines it could fly even higher if not for the air's resistance, Plato, in his lack of respect for the claims of empiricism, leaves his philosophy ungrounded. Kant demonstrated how the rationalist-idealist's search for one truth will eventually lead to philosophical antinomies. Melville's story dramatizes one such antinomy. The narrator, in his quest for the one truth, finds himself instead engaged in an unsettling dialogue that reveals the limits of two points of view: Marianna's "realist" empiricism, which refuses to make distinctions between shadows and things-in-themselves, phenomena and noumena; and the narrator's "romantic" idealism, which arrogantly assumes it knows the distinction. The story juxtaposes, without resolution, these two irreconcilable perspectives. On a textual level, the narrator's elaborate, richly allusive prose with its dominant trope of personification mediating all the descriptions of nature through imagery drawn from the span of the Western cultural tradition, stands in sharp contrast to the stark details of Marianna's story of her struggle to survive on the frontier of nature and culture in this inhospitably sublime setting. Melville does not dismiss or condescend to Marianna's point of view. If Marianna is "deluded" about "reality," she is no more so than the narrator is. She may appear to lack flexibility of perspective (in keeping with her empiricism) when she refuses to accept the possibility that her roof appears "gilded" from a distance like his appears to her; on the other hand, she may be simply rejecting his figurative use of the word *gilded* as an aestheticized misrepresentation of her economic condition, and in that sense, a lie.

This encounter on the mountain top between the first-person narrator and Marianna invites comparison with another encounter set against sublime scenery: that between Victor and the creature in Mary Shelley's *Frankenstein*. In both encounters the previously dominant first-person narrative is interrupted by a counternarrative told in first person by one cast as "other" in terms of gender or monstrosity. This narrative tells a detailed story of life on the margins of representation. In each case there is a discontinuous but linked relation between the two first-person narratives in which the dominant aestheticized discourse on nature's sublimity is opposed to an experiential narrative of oppression and struggle. In Shelley's book the scene is strategically placed at the center when Victor Frankenstein journeys to the mountains to "forget" himself in "maternal nature" after the monster he has created murders his brother, William, and fatally implicates his servant, Justine. The mountainous landscape fills him "with a sublime ecstasy" that gives "wings to his soul" allowing it "to soar from the obscure world to light and joy." Victor's lyrical ecstasy is cut short by the appearance of the monster, who, exiled from the company of man, makes his home in the "caves of ice" (93, 96). In what may be Shelley's greatest achievement in the book, the monster interrupts Victor's narrative to tell his own story, a story intimately linked to the events already witnessed by the reader from Victor's perspective. For many readers, the monster's tale of suffering and struggle told with such eloquent simplicity causes a dramatic shift in sympathy—even to the point of identification with the murderous fiend. At the end of his tale, the monster asks Victor to create a female monster to help end his loneliness. Victor shares the same monomaniacal aversion to the other sex as Bannadonna and Ahab; he cannot bring himself to fulfill the monster's request for fear the two creatures will procreate.

The sublime setting in *Frankenstein* and "The Piazza" provides the foundation for a challenge to Plato's notion of "one truth." It opens the prospect to a multiplicity of perspectives and competing truths as it lays the ground for what Lyotard calls "a thought of dispersion." In "The Piazza" the conflict between Marianna and the narrator is an example of a "differend," and it resembles in structure the conflict at the heart of Kant's sublime judgment, that between the representational-empirical faculty of Imagination and Reason, the faculty responsible for thinking totality. In "The Piazza" we get two discourses representing two distinct perspectives on the same event or object in which "one side's legitimacy does not imply the other side's lack of legitimacy" (Lyotard, *Differend*, xiii, xi). Melville represents this conflict on several levels. In aesthetic terms it is a conflict between romanticism and realism; in philosophical terms, between idealism and empiricism. Highlighting the differences between the characters in economic class and gender, Melville calls attention to the socioeconomic determinations of the conflict as well. By representing the conflict between empiricism and rational idealism as a dialogue between two individuals rather than as a split within the subject as Kant does, Melville moves beyond Kant's individualist focus to direct our attention to social, economic, and biological determinants. Despite the overwhelming power of these determinants in Marianna's case, her freedom and dignity as a human being are preserved as we experience, along with the narrator, the limits to our powers of representing her.

The conflict between the two perspectives, like the conflict between the faculties of Imagination and Reason in Kant's sublime, is not reducible to one. Melville's image for this irreducible difference is of two hop vines outside Marianna's window, which climbing their separate poles and "gaining their tip-ends, would have then joined over in an upward clasp, but the baffled shoots, groping awhile in empty air, trailed back whence they sprung." Although the perspectives of Marianna and the narrator are not to be joined together, there is a sense in which the two characters are linked through their opposition. Just as the narrator gazes longingly up at her house, she gazes down at his. They both suffer from "wakeful weariness," a condition that neither religion, nor drugs ("prayer" or the "fresh hop pillow") has been able to relieve. The narrator had hoped that by gazing on the "queen of fairies at her fairy-window" or at least "some glad mountain-girl," he would be able to "cure" his weariness (12, 6). Marianna shares the same hope about meeting the inhabitant of the "marble" house (his house) she sees in the distance—at least, that is what she tells him. Perhaps she has already guessed where the narrator comes from and is mocking his quest when she says to him, "Oh, if I could but once get to yonder house, and but look upon whoever the happy being is that lives there! A foolish thought: why do I think it? Is it that I live so lonesome, and know nothing?" (12).

The narrator cannot help but recognize himself in her words and is compelled to admit: "I, too, know nothing; and, therefore, cannot answer; but, for your sake, Marianna, well could wish that I were that happy one of the happy house you dream you see; for then you would behold him now, and, as you say, this weariness might leave you" (12). The narrator may be trying to preserve her "illusions," as some critics have suggested (see, for example, Fisher, 26). On the other hand, Marianna may be testing his mettle to see if he will reveal himself. Perhaps they both know the other knows who they are, but choose to emphasize their sense of isolation by indirect allusion. The communication seems rather one-sided as he listens to her story, but never directly reveals his identity to her.

Swearing off all future trips to fairyland, the narrator retreats to the comforts of his middle-class existence, where from his piazza, his "box-royal," the "scenery is magical—the illusion so complete." It appears that one of the literary effects of his encounter with Marianna is a shift away from the dominant pictorial trope of the opening sequence to the dramatic trope at the end—perhaps signifying a respect for the autonomy of Marianna's voice. From the deck of his piazza, he listens to the song of "Madam Meadow Lark," his own "prima donna." "And drinking in her sunrise note, which, Memnon-like, seems struck from the golden window, how far from me the weary face behind it." The narrator appropriates Marianna for the moment through his personification of the singing bird, his art-servant, but only while the sun shines on the stage of his "amphitheatre." "Every night," he tells the reader, "when the curtain falls, truth comes in with darkness. No light shows from the mountain. To and fro I walk the piazza deck, haunted by Marianna's face, and many as real a story" (12).

Marianna's face and real story ultimately resist appropriation as objects of the narrator's romantic quest for the ideal. On the level of interpretive practice, the character of Marianna also resists totalization as an object of the reader's interpretation. In contrast to the narrator, she reveals so much of her personal life, yet remains inexplicable. She can appear in various lights as clever, strong, condescending, naive, pitiful, admirable, ordinary, a fake, a fairy queen, a sorceress, an artist . . . the list seems endless. Through this indeterminacy, Melville marks the limits to his powers of representation. Along the sublime frontier, the possibility of his female character's freedom and dignity is preserved while giving the reader the opportunity to experience her own freedom in facing the limits to representation.

10

AFTERWORD

MELVILLE TAKES HIS READERS to the limits of representation so they can reflect on the political implications of their interpretive choices. Readers of "The Piazza" can choose to interpret Marianna as crazy, for example, or they can choose to interpret her as strong; ultimately, however, there is not enough textual evidence to support any one definitive interpretation. Melville's refusal to cross over this line, even in sympathy for her, is a sign of respect for the other's autonomy. The sublime feeling of respect is more important than sympathy in this case. Sympathy can end in self-satisfaction and complacency, or in a sense of one's own victimization that perpetuates the status quo. Melville's art is a response to the voice from the margins that states simply, "More than sympathy, I want your respect." The foundation of this respect lies in the experience of limits. The limit to our powers of appropriation and representation not only allows the other's autonomy and self-determination, it guarantees our own.

Melville's texts refuse the totalitarian impulse to extend the empire and colonize the other; they do not, however, refuse the quest for totality itself. The quest leads to the limits of representation. *Moby-Dick* and *Pierre* explore two ways of relating to those limits. The fanatic simply ignores them, collapsing distinctions between subject and object, empirical phenomena and ideas. On the allegorical level of reading, fanaticism's monomania shuts down the process of semantic generation. A rejection of fanaticism's egoistic transgression need not entail a rejection of ideas in general, however. I share Germaine de Staël's concern that the "terrible events" we have witnessed can leave us with "souls blasè" eager in our cynicism to dissociate ourselves from the realm of ideas when faced with the "omnipotence of actions" *(Marginalia,* 664). The enthusiast's utopian impulse needs to be tempered—not abandoned— by a sober refusal to cross over.

The lesson can be extended to our critical practice. It reminds us not to focus all of our political energy on the level of representation alone. This book grew in a critical climate of conflict between historicism and theory. One of my major intentions has been to mediate between theory and history as I meditate on the problems of affinity and influence. I am concerned that we become enslaved by the search for one to one correspondences and verifiable causal relations. Though I acknowledge the value of such factual support, I explore the limits of our historical quest as we come face to face with the historical totality that is ultimately beyond representation, what Hayden White calls the "historical sublime." This book preserves the record of an ahistorical encounter between Melville and Kant. This record represents my passion for critical interdiscourse.

As a woman in Melville studies, I sometimes feel like I am invading what has been for the most part an exclusive men's club. I cross gender lines in this case for the sake of class, not to forsake my gendered allegiances. I extend multiculturalism to include class, gender, and sexuality, along with ethnicity. Melville's texts provide a setting from which to reflect on all these aspects of our culture and ourselves. In refusing fanaticism, these texts open a sublime space. I was amazed to find a place for me there because the idea of Melville's womanless texts had always repulsed me. I imagine it is this same horror, the fear of a womanless world, that drove Shelley to write *Frankenstein.* I needed Shelley's text for support in my journey through the all-male world of *Moby-Dick,* as I believe Melville needed it to build a bridge from *Moby-Dick* to *Pierre* and "The Piazza."

These texts represent to me a new democratic style of literature, a style found in contemporary ethnographic texts that reflect on their own limits while attempting to give voice to the other.[1] Melville's texts demand a critically active and reflective reader. He is a great—and exacting—democratic teacher. H. Bruce Franklin has called him the "closest thing to a prophet we can find in the written record of [the nineteenth century]." Our job as students of his work is to "communicate the meaning of Melville's darkest visions in a world where they acquire a significance even he might not have imagined." Melville, "like any prophet worthy of the name, was not so much predicting as warning" ("President's Address," 15).

Melville may well be a prophet, but he is no saint. Like the cowardly Jonah who sought escape from the burden of his vision, Melville lived a life at odds with his literary mission. Particularly when we think of his acts of cruelty toward his family, it is difficult to reconcile the ethical wisdom of his prophecy with the actions of his person. The image of a drunken Melville beating and pushing his wife Elizabeth down a flight of stairs has imprinted itself on my mind's eye and caused me to hate him for abusing her. Whether it happened or not, I know it is possible. I know Melville could be cruel to his family. His daughter tells of being humiliated by him when as a child she extolled the virtues of a neighbor's land and he sarcastically dubbed her "little Miss Property" (Metcalf, 254). I can hear him saying this and my heart goes out to his bewildered, long suffering family. Herman Melville may be the "hero of the Melville society," but to those he lived with, he was a monster—"a beast" (Renker, 130, 127). I do not think we can separate Melville from his texts. We need no heroes, however, to communicate the meaning of his prophetic vision.

Melville's vision was a horrible one shaped in part by his experience of class and cultural conflict and injustice. He came of age in a great economic depression. He ran from his family to cavort with cannibals on the outer edge of the western empire—only to return to "Home and Mother," where he entrenched himself for life *(Typee,* 328). He trafficked among the literary elite and socially connected. He lived in close quarters with the ideological enemy and was pressed by the great historical forces of slavery, war, industrial imperialism, and the oppression of women. Melville's vision alienated him from all segments of society. From his tortured ambivalence, he found solace in his lonely craft.

A prophet sees seeds of the distopic future in the present and calls on the people to change their ways. In the prophet's warning are contained the seeds of visionary hope, the idea of a perfect community. As dark as Melville's vision is, it bids us to dream, to create out of the myriad of possibilities the art of democracy.

NOTES

1 THE ART OF DEMOCRACY

1. This rather arbitrary list reflects my own personal interests in addition
to my perception of current needs in Melville studies. Although I am interested in Melville's treatment of race and ethnicity from the perspective of a
democratic aesthetic, I defer to the excellent and comprehensive work done by
Carolyn Karcher in *Shadow over the Promised Land.*

2. It is my intention in this book to introduce pertinent new material to
be used in evaluating Melville as a political writer. Recent treatments of Melville's politics can be divided into two opposing camps: those like Wai-chee
Dimock and Larry Reynolds who characterize Melville as a political conserva-
tive, and those like Carolyn Karcher, Michael Rogin, H. Bruce Franklin, and
David Reynolds who stress his more subversive democratic leanings.

3. My task is to trace the ethical-political implications of the limits to our
powers of representation in *Moby-Dick, Pierre,* and several of the short stories.
As early as *Typee,* Melville marks the limits to representation in this spirit of
multiculturalism when his narrator states his "inability to gratify any curiosity
that may be felt with regard to the theology of the valley" (236). Of the religious ceremonies, he writes, "I saw everything, but could comprehend nothing" (244). Melville's answer in *Typee* to the fanaticism behind the missionaries'
textual fabrications is not merely to counter their reports with more "accurate"
information, but to direct attention to the constructed nature of representation itself. See T. Walter Herbert's *Marquesan Encounters* for comparisons of
the missionaries' discourse with Melville's in *Typee.*

2 MELVILLE'S KANT

1. Melville may have found a source for this particular contrast between
fanaticism and enthusiasm in Coleridge (30–33). Germaine de Staël is another
writer who contrasted the fanatic with the enthusiast in the spirit of Kant. Her
Germany was widely available in translation at this time.

2. More attention is being focused on the importance of their philosophical

discussions particularly for the writing of *Moby-Dick*. See Sanford Marovitz's essay "More Chartless Voyaging: Melville and Adler at Sea." See also Bryant, *Companion*, 45. Henry Pochmann writes in *German Culture in America* that "rightly or wrongly interpreted, Kant furnished Melville with the backbone upon which to build his anatomy of despair" (439). See also Pochmann, *German Culture*, 437.

3. Goldman calls Kant the "most profound and the most advanced thinker" of the "individualist culture of the classical bourgeoisie" (26–27). He finds it "tragic," however, that Kant, although clearly perceiving the limits of bourgeois individualist thought, remained within its "framework" (26–27, 170).

3 ARTIST OF THE SUBLIME

1. Rob Wilson's *American Sublime* illustrates the persistence of this tradition throughout American cultural history.

2. According to Elizabeth McKinsey, a history of American painting could be written around these two icons of the sublime, with Washington representing the moral sublime of the eighteenth century and Niagara Falls representing the natural sublime of the nineteenth century. (In the early twentieth century, the Brooklyn Bridge stands as the icon of the technological sublime [McKinsey, 2].)

3. It is the experience of this disjuncture between signifier and signified that Thomas Weiskel determines, from a semiotic perspective, to be the experience of the sublime (17).

4. Gary Lee Stonum notes in Emily Dickinson's sublime the same refusal to cross over into the transcendent and discusses this refusal in ethical terms. Dickinson's challenge is to find a way to circumvent the "otherwise deep complicity between sublimity and mastery" without "giving up on the experiential intensity she values or the promise of transcendence that the sublime always holds out" (68, 77). Dickinson's sublime as represented by Stonum is comparable to Melville's. I would challenge, however, Stonum's assumption of the sublime's inherent complicity with mastery.

5. Moore also notes this iconic significance in these two paintings (122).

6. Burke provides an interesting contrast to Melville. Burke's reactionary politics is reflected in his devalorization of the sublime in favor of the beautiful. The rhetoric of sublimity permeates his denunciation of the French Revolution. See Hayden White (130), and Neal Wood's "Aesthetic Dimension of Burke's Political Thought."

7. Just as the gam with the German ship reveals the philosophical shortcomings of unlimited idealism, the gam with the English ship reveals the limits

of the empirical philosophy Melville associated with England as it highlights the problem of perspective in determining the truth.

8. All biblical citations are from the Authorized (King James) Version.

9. The image of the "blank" palm appears near the end of *Moby-Dick* when Starbuck pleads with Ahab to cease his mad quest "in Jesus' name"—the only mention of Jesus in the book—and Ahab responds, "But in this matter of the whale, be the front of thy face to me as the palm of this hand—a lipless, unfeatured blank" (561).

10. Longinus writes of the sublimity of the Jewish concept of God: "So too the lawgiver of the Jews, no ordinary person, having formed a high conception of the power of the Divine Being, gave expression to it when at the very beginning of his Laws he wrote: 'God said'—what? 'Let there be light, and there was light; let there be land, and there was land' " (111).

4   THE LIMITS OF TYPOLOGY

1. Disregard for the traditional renaissance perspectival system by American artists' questing for the sublime is also to be found in the next American art movement to command international attention, Abstract Expressionism.

2. David Reynolds's *Beneath the American Renaissance* is useful for a sense of Melville's egalitarian approach to popular genres.

3. Keller lists among the "disaffected" authors Melville, Poe, Hawthorne, Dickinson, and Twain (296).

4. Yehuda T. Radday in "Chiasmus in Hebrew Biblical Narrative" writes that although the Jews "always felt the book to be exceptional, [they never] based their argument on its literary superiority." Radday finds it "therefore paradoxical that the first evidence of such appreciation [that is, the rediscovery of parallelism] is probably not older than two hundred years and due to R. Lowth, a Gentile." Radday notes that Lowth's discovery was preceded by Azariah de Rossi (ca. 1511–ca. 1578). Radday also suggests that "Jewish literati living among the Arabs must certainly have been aware of the sophisticated Arab analysis of poetry. Chiasm was one of the many forms which parallelism took in Arab poetry and prose" (cited in Roston, 50, 113 n. 1).

5. James Duban is sensitive to the fascistic implications of typological practice and covenant theology in *Moby-Dick*. I do not share his view, however, of Ishmael's complicity with such structures (see, for example, Duban, 102, 108).

5 FANATICISM

1. See Krieger's introduction to Lyotard's essay "Judiciousness in Dispute." Lyotard, he writes, distrusts "closure as a totalizing act that masks a totalitarian act" (3). Lyotard's reading of the political implications of Kant's philosophy and aesthetic of the sublime is related to my reading of fanaticism and the sublime in *Moby-Dick*. In addition to Lyotard's writings on Kant's philosophy and the sublime, see David Caroll's chapter on Lyotard, "The Aesthetic and the Political," in *Paraesthetics* where Caroll concludes that for Lyotard the aesthetics of the sublime is "a kind of critical safeguard against the dogmatism of the theoretical in general. The sublime serves to push philosophy and politics into a reflexive, critical mode, to defer indefinitely the imposition of an end on the historical-political process" (183).

2. For a recent reading of this contrast between Ishmael-Ahab, see Ronald E. Martin, *American Literature and the Destruction of Knowledge*.

3. Stanley Cavell calls this the "most subtle philosophical settlement in the modern period." Subsequent settlements, he writes, "have not displaced it, or rather, they have only displaced it." According to Cavell, "romantic texts" are characterized by the continuous "monitoring of this settlement" (31). Lyotard proposes that we all be on guard to preserve the distinctions between such heterogeneous realms as Kant delineates in the antinomies ("Judiciousness in Dispute," 27–28, 64–65).

4. Larzer Ziff, for example, calls Starbuck a "model democrat" (272).

5. Kant's categorical imperative urging us to treat one another never simply as a means, but always at the same time as an end can serve as an antidote to Ahab's utilitarian individualism. Lucian Goldman emphasizes the value of this imperative in Kant's critique of bourgeois social order's tendency "to destroy or at least to disguise all community between individuals." By focusing on Kant's notion of totality, Goldman finds the roots of a new philosophy of community in which "supreme value" is "humanity in the person of each individual man—not just the individual, as in rationalism, nor just the totality in its different forms (God, state, nation, class), as in all the romantic and intuitionist doctrines, but the *human* totality, *the community embracing the whole of humanity* and its expression in *the human person*" (Goldman, 149, 176–77).

6 PORTRAIT OF THE ENTHUSIAST

1. Ronald A. Knox and Susie I. Tucker have also written useful studies of the concept of enthusiasm. For other readings of enthusiasm in *Pierre,* see Murray Krieger, *The Tragic Vision,* and Mark Duban, *Melville's Major Fiction* (179).

2. Among prochoice advocates, for example, anti-abortionists are called "fanatical" for insisting that a "fertilized egg" is a "baby." In the popular press, Iran's Ayatollah Khomeini was called "fanatical" for issuing a death warrant against Rushdie for writing a "blasphemous" book.

3. Melville writes of de Staël: "It is delightful as well as wonderful to see— passim—such penetration of understanding in a woman, who at the same time possesses so femininely emotional a nature.—Who would one compare Madame De Staël too?—Mrs. Browning?—Mrs B. was a great woman, but Madame De S. was a greater" (Leyda, 651).

4. That Corinne was considered a model of enthusiasm is suggested by poet Maria Jewsbury's imitation of *Corinne* titled "The History of an Enthusiast." *Corinne* had an enormous influence on writers in the nineteenth century, as Ellen Moers shows in her chapter from *Literary Women* "The Myth of Corinne" (173–210).

5. Madame de Staël had seen Isabel Pellegrine captivate an audience in 1804 and 1805 (Moers, 184).

6. See de Staël, *An Extraordinary Woman*, 323. I use two sources in citing passages from the essays on enthusiasm in de Staël's *Germany:* the text above and, when possible, the excerpts printed from Melville's own copy in *Melville's Marginalia*.

7. Nancy Craig Simmons notes this ambivalence, but ultimately situates Melville's portrait of enthusiasm in the more negative empirical philosophical tradition.

8. William H. Shurr's reading of the poem also collapses the distinction between the fanatic and the enthusiast, but it is more sensitive to Melville's sympathy with the enthusiast's position (162).

9. Marc Shell writes perceptively of the radical democrat's transgression and the "ideal of universal siblinghood" in his book *The End of Kinship*: *Pierre* "moves from the commonplace romantic topos of individual brother-sister incest toward the incorporation and transcendence of incest and its taboo in a secularized Universal Siblinghood" (21).

7   ISABEL AND THE VALORIZATION OF MUSIC

1. See M. H. Abrams's *Mirror and the Lamp*. John Neubauer, in *The Emancipation of Music from Language*, attributes the inversion in the hierarchy of the arts in the latter part of the eighteenth century to the emergence of classical instrumental music: The "struggle to legitimize instrumental music became the first, decisive battle about non-representational art [and served] as a breaking ground for abstract art" (2).

2. So Herbert Schueller argues in his essay "Immanuel Kant and the Aesthetic of Music": Music is sublime "because it is the least 'graspable' and the most abstract of the arts. It can give one the feeling that it is beyond form. It can give the feeling of the formless, of the discrepancies of the parts, in Kant's terms, especially if it is the feeling of the occasion, not the form itself, which defines sublimity" (245).

3. See also Flibbert, *Melville and the Art of Burlesque,* 134.

4. Hamlet says:

And if thou prate of mountains, let them throw
Millions of acres on us, till our ground,
Singeing his pate against the burning zone
Make Ossa like a wart! Nay, and thou'lt mouth I'll rant as well as thou.

(5.1.279–83)

The affinities with Nietzsche's text are striking, as noted by Murray Krieger in *Tragic Vision* (198). Nietzsche links the Dionysian with the Titanic, calling Prometheus the "mask of the original hero, Dionysus." Nietzsche also notes a relationship between Hamlet and the Dionysian (73, 60).

8 THE "TINHORN" REBELLION

1. For example, *Critical Essays on Melville's "Pierre,"* Higgins and Parker, eds., contains at least fourteen references to melodrama in *Pierre.* Charvat writes in more detail about these melodramatic elements in his essay "Melville and the Common Reader" in *The Profession of Authorship in America, 1800–1870:*

So far as these bare bones of plot reveal, the formula, except for the unhappy ending, derives from current melodrama and the "misery novel" as developed by Mrs. Rowson and her imitators. Isabel's history serves as the theme of the long-lost child. There are overtones from the current mass fiction; the "wholesome country–wicked city" myth, the theme of the permanent "ruin" suffered by the once-seduced girl. And occasionally Melville's language rhythms drop to the level of popular melodrama. Delly is "forever ruined through the cruel arts of Ned," thinks Pierre; and "Her father will not look upon her; her mother, she hath cursed her to her face," says Isabel. (251)

For more recent discussions of melodrama in *Pierre* see Paul McCarthy (80) and Bruce Greenberg (125–26).

2. Lewis Mumford, for example, in noting Melville's "unfortunate lapse" in the "disproportion between stimulus and effect," cites Glen's rejection of Pierre as straight from the pages of "crude melodrama" (Higgins and Parker, eds.,

Critical Essays, 140). Warner Berthoff in *The Example of Melville* calls *Pierre* a "confused and maladroit exercise in the popular conventions of Romantic melodrama" (15). Matthiessen thinks Melville was so "hopelessly open to his emotions" in writing *Pierre* that he "could not find language distinguishable from that of the magazine shocker" (Higgins and Parker, eds., 208). Murray Krieger writes that the "shocking melodramatic style and action" in *Pierre* are "beyond excuse or apology" (*Tragic Vision,* 135).

3. For examples of critics supporting the idea of satire, see Edgar A. Dryden (129); Neal L. Tochlin (140); William Braswell, in Higgins and Parker, eds., *Critical Essays* (212). Charvat comes closest to taking Melville's melodrama seriously when he proposes that Melville had "hoped to invest the common formula with dignity and meaning" (251). I use the term *melodrama* in the sense of a mode rooted in, but not limited to, the popular stage melodramas of the late eighteenth and early nineteenth centuries. Peter Brooks demonstrates in *The Melodramatic Imagination* how several nineteenth-century novelists incorporated melodramatic elements in their works. Although the melodramatic mode is central to Melville's *Pierre,* the book is not to be reduced to melodrama. It encompasses melodrama (along with other modes as well) and is much more than its melodramatic parts.

4. Writing from a psychoanalytic perspective, Eric Bentley concludes that melodrama is "not so much exaggerated as uninhibited." Its excessively artificial rhetoric represents a "victory over repression" (198). For other psychoanalytic approaches to melodrama, see Peter Brooks and Laura Mulvey.

5. David Reynolds convincingly demonstrates Melville's debt to popular culture. "It was Melville's democratic openness to wild forces within his contemporary popular culture that distinguished him from his more snobbish literary colleagues" (276–77).

6. At a 1988 MLA session on nineteenth-century American literature, Reynolds had to defend himself against the attacks of feminists who objected to his condescending treatment of "sentimental" women writers in *Beneath the American Renaissance.*

In order to understand Melville's "social vision," Carolyn Karcher proposes that we situate his works not in relation to Hawthorne and Poe, but in relation to contemporary protest writers like Frederick Douglass, Harriet Beecher Stowe, and Rebecca Harding Davis—writers, I would add, indebted to the rhetoric of early political melodrama (see Karcher's notes to *Instructor's Guide for the Heath Anthology of American Literature,* 237). See also Booth for a discussion of the subversive "anti-authoritarianism" in early melodrama (63–64).

7. See Brooks (85). Michael Booth's *English Melodrama* traces parallel developments in the English theater. The Licensing Act of 1737 confined "legitimate" drama to theaters holding royal patents. Until the patent privileges were abol-

ished in 1843, "anyone wishing to offer dramatic entertainment inside the law but outside the patent houses had to content himself with dumbshow, music, and spectacle" (Booth, 52–53).

8. One of the originators of melodrama, Pixerecourt, said he "aimed his plays at an unlettered populace." See Booth, 44–45, and Rahill, xviii.

9. The novels by Cooper that deal with the controversy are *Sartostoe, Little-page Tales, Chainbearer,* and *Redskins.* Walt Whitman, writing for the *Brooklyn Eagle,* called the Anti-Renters "the most violent faction which has disgraced the State since laws were heard of in this hemisphere." Whitman wrote in support of the election of Silas Wright and against the Anti-Renter candidate, John Gay, "whose hope and success," according to Whitman, "mainly depends upon his supposed sympathy with a spirit of social disorganization and rebellion." See Henry Christman, 275.

For information about Marie Gansevoort's link to the patroons, see Henry Murray's introduction and explanatory notes for *Pierre* (435–36). The story of Melville's support for the Anti-Renters provides a needed supplement to Michael Rogin's work in *Subversive Genealogy.* It can help qualify Rogin's thesis that the "crisis of bourgeois society at mid-century . . . entered [American] politics by way of slavery and race rather than class" (xi).

Douglas Jerrold, a writer from the underclasses who dreamed of a national drama that would reflect the times, claimed to have invented domestic melo-drama (see Frank Rahill, 161–62). Jerrold is an interesting figure to consider in relation to Melville. Melville may have known of Jerrold's very favorable review of *Typee* (see Melville, *Journal,* 147). Melville writes enthusiastically of seeing two different productions of Douglas Jerrold's *Housekeeper* during his trip to London in 1849 (see Leyda, 326, 348). Several critics have noted the influence of Jerrold's nautical melodramas on the writing of *Billy Budd* (see, for example, B. R. McElderry, and Rita and Richard Gollin).

10. From the *New York Sun,* 16 August 1852. See Higgins and Parker, eds., *Critical Essays,* 35.

11. Ainge Devyr, an Irish activist in the Chartist movement who joined the struggle of the Anti-Renters in 1842, noted that at that time "the people were being crushed by a land monopoly on the one hand and a growing industrial economy on the other" (Christman, 50). Douglas Miller describes increased social stratification after 1830, due primarily to the influx of immigrants who formed a working class for the rising industrial-capital economy (78–79). The one exception to the rise of the aristocracy during this time was the landed gentry of the Hudson Valley, who were becoming land poor because of the in-creased importance of the urban centers (Miller, 60, 78–79, 62).

12. Karcher writes that Pierre confuses "family pride with patriotism" (94).

9   ALONG SUBLIME FRONTIERS: A WOMAN'S STORY

1. See essays by Bette S. Weidman, Lucy M. Freibert, Lea Bertani Vozar Newman, and Laurie Robertson-Lorant.

2. One could also trace a trajectory touching on a similar configuration substituting race for gender, which would end perhaps in *Benito Cereno* (see Karcher), or substituting sexuality and culminating in *Billy Budd* (see Robert K. Martin, *Hero, Captain, and Stranger*).

3. Even if we add "Bartleby" and *Billy Budd* to the list of texts commonly taught, we are still going to find a dearth of women characters.

4. See Robyn Wiegman, for a reading of Melville's critique of the "ideological structures of gender, class, and race underlying the male bond" in *Moby-Dick* (735).

5. For an exposition of this concept of genre, see Rosalie L. Colie.

6. In a letter to his publisher, Richard Bentley, Melville writes that his new book possesses "unquestionable novelty, as regards my former ones" and treats "of utterly new scenes & characters." He assures Bentley that it is "very much more calculated for popularity than anything you have yet published of mine—being a regular romance, with a mysterious plot to it, & stirring passions at work, and withall, representing a new and elevated aspect of American life" (*Letters,* 150).

Melville's earlier "inarticulate" female characters include the mute woman in "Fragments from a Writing Desk, No. 2," Fayaway in *Typee* (who speaks, but not in a language the narrator understands), and Yillah in *Mardi.* All represent love objects of the hero.

7. In 1986 Joyce Sparer Adler and the Melville Society attempted to redress the problem by publishing papers on "Women in Melville's Art" delivered during the Modern Language Association conference. See *Melville Society Extracts,* no. 65 (February 1986): 2–16.

8. See for example Joyce Warren in *The American Narcissus.*

9. Hershel Parker during the 1988 Melville session of the Northeast Modern Language Association cited evidence to suggest that Melville did indeed write Agatha's story, but that the story has not yet been found.

10. Hawthorne, after reading *Ruth Hall,* amended his previous remark about the "damned mob of scribbling women." He wrote that Fanny Fern

> writes as if the devil was in her; and that is the only condition under which a woman ever writes anything worth reading. Generally women write like emasculated men, and are only distinguished from male authors by the greater feebleness and folly; but when they throw off the restraints

of decency, and come before the public stark naked, as it were; then their
books are sure to possess character and value. (*Letters of Hawthorne to
William Ticknor,* 78)

11. Gillian Brown, in *Domestic Individualism,* for example, claims Melville
hated sentimentalism (135).

12. Certainly the omission of an ultimately optimistic view makes for a world
of difference between the two books. Unlike Stowe, Melville is interested in
the limits of the sentimental–melodramatic vision (as he was interested in the
limits to the romantic quest in *Moby-Dick*). However, I suggest that this interest in limits does not preclude an earnest engagement with the sentiment and
rhetoric of melodrama.

13. Melville purchased these two books while in London before writing
Moby-Dick (Leyda, 351).

14. Naomi Schor analyzes the gendered implications of the aesthetic tension
between realist and sublime aesthetics in *Reading in Detail.* David Simpson
notes the historical "coincidence" linking the expansion of empire and capital with the rhetoric of sublimity. There is "something ethically uncomfortable
at the heart of our craving for bigness and our urge to set ourselves against
enormity in a process of cognizance or conquest, whether of depth, space or
territory" (246). For similar critiques of the politic of sublimity, see Rob Wilson on the Whitmanic sublime and Wai-Chee Dimock's reading of Melville's
rhetoric of empire and expansion. From a feminist perspective, Naomi Schor
reads the totalizing thrust in much sublime rhetoric as indicative of a "masculinist aesthetic" (22).

15. For a discussion of the feminist and ethical implications behind the rejection of beauty, see Mary Wollstonecraft, for whom beauty is a mere arbitrary
power, an accident of birth, which will keep women enslaved until they ab-
jure its decadent and intoxicating power (*Vindication of the Rights of Woman,*
chap. 2). See also Paul Mattick, Jr., for a reading of Wollstonecraft's critique of
beauty and valorization of the sublime (299–300).

AFTERWORD

1. See James Clifford's lucid and compelling *The Predicament of Culture*
for reflections on twentieth-century ethnography and the arts. I admit I have
found traces of this "new" style in Montaigne, Shakespeare, and even Homer,
all of whom mark the limits to representation in respect for cultural others.
Perhaps this new world of democratic literature is just new to me.

WORKS CITED

Abrams, M. H. *The Mirror and the Lamp: Romantic Theory and the Critical Tradition.* New York: Oxford University Press, 1953.

Auerbach, Erich. "Figura." In *Drama of European Literature.* Minneapolis: University of Minnesota press, 1984.

Baldick, Chris. *In Frankenstein's Shadow: Myth Monstrosity and Nineteenth-Century Writing.* Oxford: Clarendon Press, 1987.

Baym, Nina. "Melville's Quarrel with Fiction." *PMLA* 94 (October 1979): 909–23.

Bentley, Eric. "Melodrama." In *Tragedy: Vision and Form,* edited by Robert Corrigan, 193–204. New York: Harper and Row, 1981.

Bercovitch, Sacvan. *The American Jeremiad.* Madison: University of Wisconsin Press, 1978.

Berthoff, Warner. *The Example of Melville.* Princeton: Princeton University Press, 1962.

Bloch, Ernst. *The Principle of Hope.* Translated by Neville Plaice, Stephen Plaice, and Paul Knight. Cambridge: MIT Press, 1986.

Booth, Michael. *English Melodrama.* London: Herbert Jenkins, 1965.

Breinig, Helmbrecht. "The Destruction of Fairyland: Melville's 'Piazza' in the Tradition of the American Imagination." *ELH* 35 (1968): 254–83.

Brodtkorb, Paul, Jr. *Ishmael's White World: A Phenomenological Reading of 'Moby Dick.'* New Haven: Yale University Press, 1965.

Brooks, Peter. *The Melodramatic Imagination: Balzac, Henry James, Melodrama, and the Mode of Excess.* New York: Columbia University Press, 1985.

Brown, Gillian. *Domestic Individualism: Imagining Self in Nineteenth-Century America.* Berkeley & Los Angeles: University of California Press, 1990.

Brumm, Ursula. *American Thought and Religious Typology.* Translated by John Hooglund. New Brunswick: Rutgers, 1970.

Bryant, John. *A Companion to Melville Studies.* Westport, Conn.: Greenwood Press, 1986.

———. "Herman Melville: A Prospective." *Melville Society Extracts,* no. 88 (March 1992): 10–14.

Caroll, David. *Paraesthetics: Foucault, Lyotard, Derrida.* New York: Methuen, 1987.

Charvat, William. *The Profession of Authorship in America, 1800–1870.* Edited by Matthew J. Bruccoli. Columbus: Ohio State University Press, 1968.

Christman, Henry. *Tin Horns and Calico: A Decisive Episode in the Emergence of Democracy.* New York: Henry Holt, 1945.

Clifford, James. *The Predicament of Culture: Twentieth-Century Ethnography, Literature, and Art.* Cambridge: Harvard University Press, 1988.

Coleridge, Samuel Taylor. *The Collected Works of Samuel Taylor Coleridge.* Vol. 1. Edited by James Engell and Walter Jackson Bate. Princeton: Princeton University Press, 1983.

Colie, Rosalie. *The Resources of Kind: Genre Theory in the Renaissance.* Edited by Barbara K. Lewalski. Berkeley: University of California Press, 1973.

Cowan, Bainard. *Exiled Waters: Moby-Dick and the Crisis of Allegory.* Baton Rouge: Louisiana State University Press, 1982.

DeLeuze, Gilles. *Kant's Critical Philosophy.* Translated by Hugh Tomlinson and Barbara Habberjam. London: Athlone Press, 1984.

Dimock, Wai-chee. *Empire for Liberty: Melville and the Poetics of Individualism.* Princeton: Princeton University Press, 1989.

Donovan, Josephine. *New England Local Color Literature.* New York: Ungar, 1983.

Douglas, Ann. *The Feminization of American Culture.* New York: Knopf, 1977.

Dryden, Edgar A. *Melville's Thematics of Form: The Great Art of Telling the Truth.* Baltimore: Johns Hopkins University Press, 1968.

Duban, James. *Melville's Major Fiction: Politics, Theology, and Imagination.* DeKalb: Northern Illinois University Press, 1983.

Eagleton, Terry. *The Ideology of the Aesthetic.* Oxford: Basil Blackwell, 1990.

Emerson, Ralph Waldo. *Collected Works.* Vol. 3. Cambridge: Harvard University Press, 1987.

———. *The Early Lectures of Ralph Waldo Emerson.* Edited by Robert E. Spiller and Stephen E. Whicher. Vol. 1. Cambridge: Harvard University Press, 1964.

Feidelson, Charles. *Symbolism and American Literature.* Chicago: University of Chicago Press, 1953.

Fetterly, Judith. Introduction to *Provisions.* Bloomington: Indiana University Press, 1985.

Fiedler, Leslie. *What Was Literature? Class Culture and Mass Society.* New York: Simon and Schuster, 1982.

Fisher, Marvin. *Going Under: Melville's Short Fiction and the American 1850s.* Baton Rouge: Louisiana State University Press, 1977.

Flibbert, Joseph. *Melville and the Art of Burlesque.* Amsterdam: Rodopi, 1974.

Franklin, H. Bruce. "Herman Melville: Artist of the Worker's World." In

Weapons of Criticism: Marxism in America and the Literary Tradition, edited by Norman Rudick, 287–309. Palo Alto, Calif.: Ramparts Press, 1976.

———. "President's Address." *Melville Society Extracts* 96 (March 1994): 14–15.

Freibert, Lucy M. "Herman Melville: The Feminine Dimension." *Melville Society Extracts,* no. 65 (February 1986): 9–11.

Glenn, Barbara. "Melville and the Sublime in *Moby-Dick.*" *American Literature* 48 (May 1976): 165–82.

Goldmann, Lucien. *Immanuel Kant.* Translated by Robert Black. London: NLB, 1971.

Gollin, Rita, and Richard Gollin. "Justice in an Earlier Treatment of the *Billy Budd* 'Theme.'" *American Literature* 28 (January 1957): 513–15.

Greenberg, Bruce. *Some Other World to Find.* Urbana: University of Illinois Press, 1989.

Grimsted, David. *Melodrama Unveiled: American Theater and Culture, 1800–1850.* Chicago: University of Chicago Press, 1968.

Hawthorne, Nathaniel. *The Letters of Hawthorne to William Ticknor, 1851–1869.* Vol. 1. Edited by C. E. Frazer Clark, Jr. Newark, N.J.: Carteret Book Club, 1972.

Hedge, Frederic H. *Prose Writers of Germany.* 1847. Reprint, Philadelphia: Carey and Hart, 1849.

Herbert, T. Walter, Jr. *Marquesan Encounters: Melville and the Meaning of Civilization.* Cambridge: Harvard University Press, 1980.

Herzog, Kirstin. *Women, Ethnics, and Exotics: Images of Power in Mid-Nineteenth-Century Fiction.* Knoxville: University of Tennessee Press, 1983.

Higgins, Brian, and Hershel Parker, eds. *Critical Essays on Melville's "Pierre."* Boston: G. K. Hall, 1983.

Higham, John. *From Boundlessness to Consolidation: The Transformation of American Culture, 1848–1860.* Ann Arbor, Mich.: William Clements Library, 1969.

Jerrold, Douglas. *The Rent Day: A Domestic Drama in Three Acts.* New York: William Taylor.

Kant, Immanuel. *Critique of Judgment.* Translated by J. H. Bernard. New York: Hafner Press, 1951.

———. *Critique of Practical Reason.* Translated by Lewis White Beck. Indianapolis: Bobbs-Merrill, 1956.

———. *Critique of Pure Reason.* Translated by Norman Kemp Smith. New York: St. Martin's Press, 1965.

Karcher, Carolyn L. "Herman Melville." In *Instructor's Guide for the Heath Anthology of American Literature.* Edited by Paul Lauter and Judith A. Stanford, 233–49. Lexington, Mass. and Toronto: D.C. Heath, 1990.

————. *Shadow over the Promised Land: Slavery, Race, and Violence in Melville's America.* Baton Rouge: Louisiana State University Press, 1980.

Keller, Karl. "Alephs, Zahirs, and the Triumph of Ambiguity: Typology in Nineteenth-Century American Literature." In *Literary Uses of Typology,* edited by Earl Miner, 274–314. Princeton: University of Princeton Press, 1977.

Kenny, Rosemary Austin. "Melville's Short Fiction: A Methodology of Unknowing." Ph.D. dissertation, University of Wisconsin, 1980.

Knox, Ronald A. *Enthusiasm: A Chapter in the History of Religion.* New York: Oxford University Press, 1961.

Krieger, Murray. "Introduction: The Literary, the Textual, the Social." In *The Aims of Representation: Subject/Text/History,* edited by Murray Krieger, 1–22. New York: Columbia University Press, 1987.

————. *The Tragic Vision: Variations on a Theme in Literary Interpretation.* New York: Holt, Rinehart, and Winston, 1960.

Leyda, Jay. *The Melville Log: A Documentary Life of Herman Melville, 1819–1891.* 2 vols. New York: Gordian Press, 1969.

Longinus. *On the Sublime.* In *Classical Literary Criticism.* Translated by T. S. Dorsch, 99–158. London: Penguin, 1965.

Lyotard, Jean-François. *The Differend: Phrases in Dispute.* Translated by Georges Van Den Abbeele. Minneapolis: University of Minnesota Press, 1988.

————. "Judiciousness in Dispute, or Kant after Marx." Translated by Cecile Lindsay. In *The Aims of Representation: Subject/Text/History,* edited by Murray Krieger, 23–67. New York: Columbia University Press, 1987.

Marovitz, Sanford. "More Chartless Voyaging: Melville and Adler at Sea." In *Studies in the American Renaissance, 1986,* edited by Joel Myerson, 373–84. Charlottesville: University of Virginia Press, 1986.

Martin, Robert K. *Hero, Captain, and Stranger: Male Friendship, Social Critique, and Literary Form in the Sea Novels of Herman Melville.* Chapel Hill: University of North Carolina Press, 1986.

Martin, Ronald E. *American Literature and the Destruction of Knowledge: Innovative Writing in the Age of Epistemology.* Durham, N.C.: Duke University Press, 1991.

Matthiessen, F. O. *American Renaissance: Art and Expression in the Age of Emerson and Whitman.* New York: Oxford University Press, 1941.

Mattick, Paul, Jr. "Beautiful and Sublime: Gender Totemism in the Constitution of Art." *Journal of Aesthetics and Art Criticism* 48, no. 4 (fall 1990): 293–303.

McCarthy, Paul. *The Twisted Mind: Madness in Herman Melville's Fiction.* Iowa City: University of Iowa Press, 1990.

McElderry, B. R. "Three Earlier Treatments of the *Billy Budd* Theme." *American Literature* 27 (May 1955): 251–57.

McKinsey, Elizabeth. *Niagara Falls: Icon of the American Sublime.* Cambridge: Cambridge University Press, 1985.

Melville, Herman. "Hawthorne and His Mosses." In *Moby-Dick,* edited by Harrison Hayford and Hershel Parker, 535–51. New York: Norton, 1967.

———. *Journal of a Visit to London and the Continent by Herman Melville, 1849–1850.* Edited by Eleanor Melville Metcalf. Cambridge: Harvard University Press, 1948.

———. *The Letters of Herman Melville.* Edited by Merrell R. Davis and William H. Gilman. New Haven: Yale University Press, 1960.

———. *Melville's Marginalia.* 2 vols. Edited by Walter Cowen. New York: Garland, 1987.

———. *Moby-Dick, or The Whale.* Edited by Harrison Hayford, Hershel Parker, and G. Thomas Tanselle. Evanston, Ill.: Northwestern University Press, 1968.

———. *The Piazza Tales and Other Prose Pieces, 1839–1860.* Edited by Harrison Hayford, Alma A. MacDougal, and G. Thomas Tanselle. Evanston, Ill: Northwestern University Press, 1987.

———. *Pierre, or the Ambiguities.* Edited by Harrison Hayford, Hershel Parker, and G. Thomas Tanselle. Evanston, Ill.: Northwestern University Press and the Newberry Library, 1971.

———. *Poems.* New York: Russell and Russell, 1963.

Melville Society Extracts, no. 65 (February 1986): 2–16.

Metcalf, Eleanor Melville. *Herman Melville: Cycle and Epicycle.* Cambridge: Harvard University Press, 1953.

Miller, Douglas. *Jacksonian Aristocracy: Class and Democracy in New York, 1830–1860.* New York: Oxford University Press, 1969.

Miller, Perry. *Errand in the Wilderness.* Cambridge: Harvard University Press, 1964.

———. *The Raven and the Whale: The War of Words and Wits in the Era of Poe and Melville.* New York: Harcourt, 1956.

Moers, Ellen. *Literary Women.* Garden City, N.Y.: Doubleday, 1976.

Moore, Richard S. *That Cunning Alphabet: Melville's Aesthetics of Nature.* Amsterdam: Rodopi, 1982.

Mulvey, Laura. "Notes on Sirk and Melodrama." *Movie,* nos. 24–26 (1976–77): 53–56.

Murray, Henry. Introduction and explanatory notes for *Pierre, or the Ambiguities,* by Herman Melville. New York: Hendricks House, 1949.

Mushabac, Jane. *Melville's Humor: A Critical Study.* Hamden, Conn.: Archon Books, 1981.

Nahm, Milton. "'Sublimity' and the 'Moral Law' in Kant's Philosophy." *Kant-Studien* 48 (1956–57): 502–24.

Neubauer, John. *The Emancipation of Music from Language: Departure from Mimesis in Eighteenth-Century Aesthetics.* New Haven: Yale University Press, 1986.

Newman, Lea Bertani Vozar. "Melville's 'Bell-Tower' Revisited: The Story of Female Revenge." *Melville Society Extracts,* no. 65 (February 1986): 11–14.

Nietzsche, Friedrich. *The Birth of Tragedy from the Spirit of Music.* Translated by William Houseman. New York: Russell and Russell, 1964

Noll, Mark A. "The Image of the United States as a Biblical Nation, 1776–1865." In *The Bible in America,* edited by Mark A. Noll and Nathan Hatch, 39–58. New York: Oxford University Press, 1982.

Pater, Walter. *The Renaissance.* New York: New American Library, 1959.

Pochmann, Henry. *German Culture in America: Philosophical and Literary Influences, 1600–1900.* Madison: University of Wisconsin Press, 1957.

Poenicke, Klaus. "A View from the Piazza: Herman Melville and the Legacy of the European Sublime." *Comparative Literature Studies* 4 (1967): 267–81.

Rahill, Frank. *The World of Melodrama.* University Park: Pennsylvania State University Press, 1967.

Renker, Elizabeth. "Herman Melville, Wife Beating, and the Written Page." *American Literature* 66 (March 1994): 123–50.

Reynolds, David S. *Beneath the American Renaissance: The Subversive Imagination in the Age of Emerson and Melville.* New York: Knopf, 1988

Reynolds, Larry J. *European Revolutions and the American Literary Renaissance.* New Haven: Yale University Press, 1988.

Robertson-Lorant, Laurie. "Melville's Embrace of the Invisible Woman." *Centennial Review* 34 (Summer 1990): 401–11.

Rogin, Michael. *Subversive Genealogy: The Politics and Art of Herman Melville.* New York: Knopf, 1983.

Roston, Murray. *Prophet and Poet.* Evanston: Northwestern University Press, 1965.

Ryan, Mary. *The Empire of Mother: American Writing about Domesticity, 1830–1860.* New York: Institute for Research in History and Haworth Press, 1982.

Sanford, Charles. *The Quest for Paradise: Europe and the American Moral Imagination.* Urbana: University of Illinois, 1961.

Schor, Naomi. *Reading in Detail: Aesthetics and the Feminine.* New York: Methuen, 1987.

Schueller, Herbert M. "Immanuel Kant and the Aesthetics of Music." *Journal of Aesthetics and Art Criticism* 14, no. 2 (December 1955): 143–247.

Sealts, Merton. *Pursuing Melville.* Madison: University of Wisconsin, 1982.

Shakespeare, William. *Hamlet.* In *The Riverside Shakespeare,* edited by G. Blakemore Evans. Boston: Houghton Mifflin, 1974.

Shell, Marc. *The End of Kinship: "Measure for Measure," Incest, and the Ideal of Universal Siblinghood.* Stanford: Stanford University Press, 1988.

Shell, Susan Meld. *The Rights of Reason: A Study of Kant's Philosophy and Politics.* Toronto: University of Toronto Press, 1980.

Shelley, Mary. *Frankenstein, or the new Prometheus.* New York: New American Library, 1965.

Shurr, William H. *The Mystery of Iniquity: Melville as Poet, 1857–1891.* Louisville: University of Kentucky Press, 1972.

Simmons, Nancy Craig. "Why an Enthusiast? Melville's *Pierre* and the Problem of the Imagination." *ESQ* 33 (3d quarter, 1987): 146–67.

Simpson, David. "Commentary: Updating the Sublime." *Studies in Romanticism* 26 (Summer 1987): 245–58.

Staël, Germaine de. *An Extraordinary Woman: Selected Writings of Germaine de Staël.* Translated by Vivian Folkenflik. New York: Columbia University Press, 1987.

———. *Germany.* New York: Kirk, 1814.

Stein, William Bysshe. *The Poetry of Melville's Later Years.* Albany: State University of New York Press, 1970.

Stonum, Gary Lee. *The Dickinson Sublime.* Madison: University of Wisconsin Press, 1991.

Tolchin, Neal L. *Mourning, Gender, and Creativity in the Art of Herman Melville.* New Haven: Yale University Press, 1988.

Tompkins, Jane. *Sensational Designs: The Cultural Work of American Fiction, 1790–1860.* New York: Oxford University Press, 1985.

Tucker, Susie I. *Enthusiasm: A Study in Semantic Change.* Cambridge: Cambridge University Press, 1972.

Warren, Joyce W. *The American Narcissus: Individualism and Women in Nineteenth-Century American Fiction.* New Brunswick, N.J.: Rutgers University Press, 1984.

Weidman, Bette S. "Women in Melville's Art: The Reader's Education in Feeling 'if he feel not he reads in vain . . .'." *Melville Society Extracts,* no. 65 (February 1986): 3–6.

Weiskel, Thomas. *The Romantic Sublime.* Baltimore: Johns Hopkins University Press, 1976.

White, Hayden. "The Politics of Historical Interpretation: Discipline and De-Sublimation." In *The Politics of Interpretation,* edited by W. J. T. Mitchell, 119–43. Chicago: University of Chicago Press, 1983.

Wiegman, Robyn. "Melville's Geography of Gender." *ALH* 1 (1989): 735–53.

Works Cited

Wilson, Rob. *American Sublime: The Genealogy of a Poetic Genre.* Madison: University of Wisconsin Press, 1991.

Wollstonecraft, Mary. *Vindication of the Rights of Woman.* New York and London: Penguin, 1985.

Wood, Neal. "The Aesthetic Dimension of Burke's Political Thought." *Journal of British Studies* 4 (1964): 41–64.

Wright, Nathalia. *Melville's Use of the Bible.* Durham, N.C.: Duke University Press, 1949.

Ziff, Larzer. *Literary Democracy: The Declaration of Cultural Independence in America.* New York: Viking Press, 1981.

Zuckert, Catherine H. *Natural Right and the American Imagination: Political Philosophy in Novel Form.* Savage, Md: Rowan and Littlefield, 1990.

INDEX